THE DELIGHTS OF
Russian
cuisine

The publishers would like to thank the
following for their assistance during the
production of this book: Oleg Kuznetsov,
Commercial Consul, Consulate General
USSR, Sydney; Henri Leuzinger,
Executive Chef and Food and Beverage
Manager, Ansett Airlines of Australia;
James Gleeson, General Manager,
Denny's Restaurants (Australia)

Published by Bay Books, 61–69 Anzac
Parade, Kensington, NSW 2033

Publisher: George Barber

National Library of Australia
Card number and ISBN 1 86256 271 7

Typesetting by Savage Type Pty Ltd
Printed in Singapore by Toppan Printing
Co.

BB88

THE DELIGHTS OF
Russian
cuisine

YVONNE WEBB

Photography ASHLEY BARBER
Styling MICHELLE GORRY

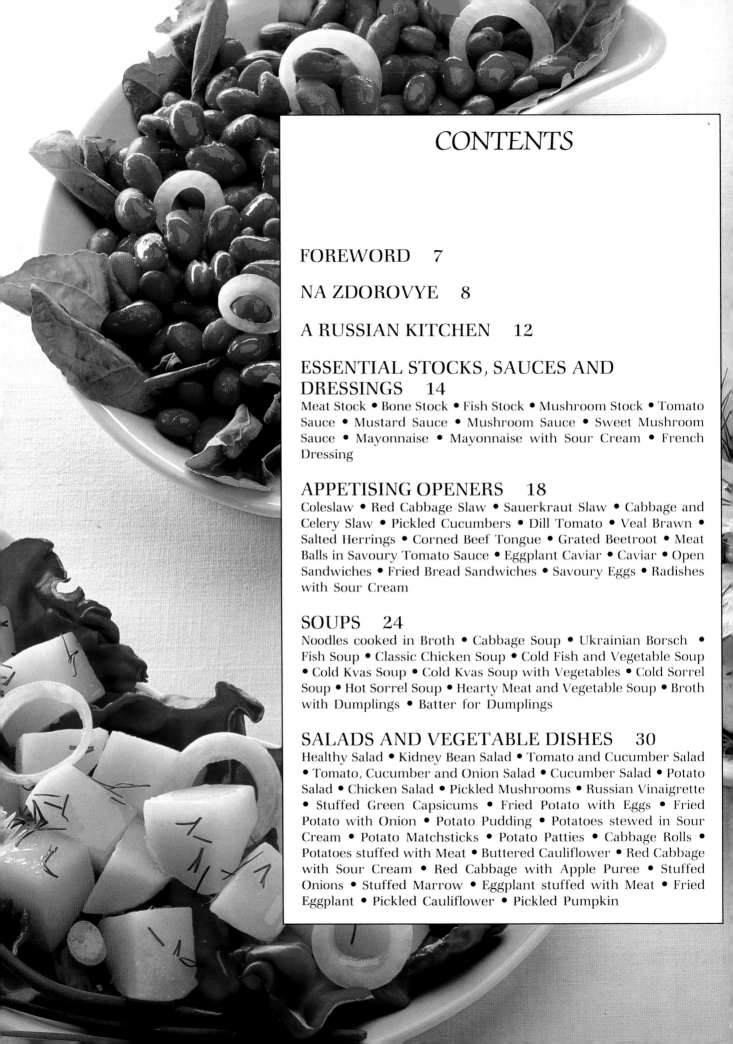

CONTENTS

FOREWORD

Russian cuisine, unlike the world famous Russian ballet, has been little known in the West until recently. Today, however, there is not only a growing awareness but enjoyment of the flavour and variety of many Russian specialities from hot and cold zakuski (the Russian word for hors d'oeuvres) to soups including okroshka and rassolnik, popular dishes such as chicken Kiev, shashlik, pelmeni, piroshki and blini and delicious desserts, cakes and sweet pastries such as kisel, Charlotte russe, and tort rooski. All food fit for a king — or as they say in Russia 'Po-tsarski!'

There have been many reasons for the growing interest in Russian food. Mine was greatly stimulated by the challenge of having to research and plan the menus for the Troika Restaurant, a feature of the Soviet Pavilion at Brisbane's World Expo '88. The Troika Restaurant, so named by the USSR Chamber of Commerce who were responsible for the Soviet Pavilion, was created and operated by Ansett Airlines. How I wish I had had Yvonne Webb's *The Delights of Russian Cuisine* to hand. It would have saved me a great deal of time researching (and tasting) the traditional specialities of Russian cooking.

Of course, when we say Russian, we are really talking about the USSR. The Soviet Union covers a vast area — in fact one-sixth of the world's surface. Climate and neighbouring countries have considerably influenced the music, art and cooking of the Soviet peoples from the icy north to the sunny shores of the Black Sea, from the culture of Europe on its western borders to Asia in the east. History, too, has played its part.

Peter the Great who reigned in Russia from the latter part of the seventeenth century formed a close association with the Prussian court and doubtless it was German barons from the Baltic provinces serving in Russia who introduced sausages, sauerkraut and schnitzels. Salami and noodles came from the days when the Italians were influential with their music, ballet and of course, cuisine. At the time of Catherine the Great, the French influence was most prominent. She enthusiastically adopted their culture, language and chefs for her court.

Out of all these influences, Russian cooking has emerged into its own. One of the main ingredients for many dishes is smetana (sour cream). It is sometimes said that too much is used. But when one considers the superb borsch , beef stroganoff, hot and cold desserts and bliny covered with it, much may be forgiven — and enjoyed. Na zdorovye.

Henri Leuzinger
Executive Chef and Food and
Beverage Manager
Ansett Airlines

NA ZDOROVYE
CHEERS

Russian food and style of cooking is not generally well-known, except perhaps through gourmet items such as caviar and Chatka crab. Many of us have tasted that famous Russian drink, vodka, but few people outside Russia have sampled the legendary commercial fruit juices and syrups.

Russian cooking, like the Russian national character, shows great diversity, is sometimes difficult, but always interesting. The Baltic states of the north favour salted fish, cabbage and lots of berries, while the Caucasian regions (such as Georgia) in the south, have developed a traditional cuisine based on lamb, shashliks and exotic fruits such as pomegranates.

Kasha or cereals, in the form of breads, pies, pastries and porridge, form the backbone of any meal. Russian breads have a wonderful flavour — once tasted, never forgotten. There is a wide selection of wheat and rye breads available, made from specially milled flour, and of all different shapes and sizes — from the large, round loaves to smaller circles of bread, like bagels. Porridge is an essential and staple part of the

Russian diet. It can be eaten at breakfast as a cereal, at lunch with fish, eggs or poultry, or as a sweet, with fresh fruit or Kisel.

Russian people demand good, and especially fresh, food. Because they tend to buy larger quantities of food at any one time than in Western countries, there is usually a rapid turnover of food in shops and markets.

Russian restaurants around the world have focused on well-known dishes such as Chicken Kiev, developing their own special if rather limited, traditional menus. Russian cuisine, however, has a superb range of dishes, among them, wonderful savoury pastries, fruit tarts, ice creams and other sweets which few people outside Russia are familiar with.

Russian cooking has traditionally had a high egg and dairy product content. This has changed, reflecting modern Russian lifestyles and health concerns. Popular family and health magazines now regularly feature articles on the importance of a balanced diet and regular exercise for a healthy lifestyle. Many of the traditional and favourite Russian dishes have been modified to suit current tastes.

Frederique Hibon: Sygma/Austral

Traditionally, the typical Russian family sits down together at the table to eat. Bread is always served with meals. Hearty soups such as Borsch, chicken soup and Okroshka (chilled vegetable soup) are very popular. Because many traditional dishes improve over time, by 'standing', Russians tend to cook a large amount and refrigerate the extra. In pre-refrigeration times, food was buried in the snow until needed! All food is placed on the table and family members help themselves. This also happens in more formal situations. In restaurants typically 'zakuski' dishes (appetisers or 'snacks') are laid out on the table, and then followed by other courses.

Russians usually have dinner (our lunch) in the middle of the day, at about 1–2 o'clock. Their dinner is a four course meal, consisting of snacks or zakuski, soup, main meal and then coffee or tea, fruit and sweets or dessert. Soup is only eaten at dinner time. The Russian evening meal is called supper, and is eaten at about 7–8 o'clock. Excluding soup, the courses follow the same pattern as at dinner.

Vodka was traditionally drunk at all meals — in thimble-sized glasses, with one swig, like schnapps. These days, vodka consumption has been cut in half, and vodka is saved, like wine, for more special occasions. Kvas, a mild, home-brewed beer, is an integral part of meals, drunk by children and adults alike. It is a refreshing, low-alcohol drink (about 1%), with many different brews available. Kvas is also sold in big barrels on street corners. In the Georgian south, red wine (with a much higher alcoholic content), is generally favoured over kvas.

Food preparation, and eating and drinking, are important Russian pastimes, and much time and effort is spent in the kitchen for special occasions. Many dishes, such as yeast pastry dishes, can be made ahead of time and frozen until needed. Russian recipes are designed to cater for large numbers, and even small families cook more food than they need, and refrigerate or freeze what's left over.

The recipes included in this book come from a range of different sources: Russian popular magazines, cookbooks, both ancient and modern, and family and friends. The recipes stand very well on their own, or can be adapted to suit different tastes and occasions. Root vegetables, such as potatoes, carrots, parsnips, turnips and onions, are the most commonly used in Russian cooking. Root vegetables have always been the most readily available in Russia, even in the harsh winters. The USSR, however, is a vast country, and in the warmer climate of the Georgian south, a much wider range of fresh produce is available all year round. A variety of fresh fruit and vegetables can be used to enhance and add colour to traditional dishes.

When Russians entertain, socialising is important, and there is much talking, laughter and even singing at the table, especially for a special occasion. Socialising can go on for a few hours, just for the zakuski let alone the other courses! As a result the temperature food is served at, is not a critical factor, and many of the dishes can be eaten hot or cold.

Both English and Russian recipe names are given. Russian names are spelled phonetically to aid pronunciation.

Dolls and bowls — New Era Bookshop

A set of traditional Russian dolls (Matryoshkas) with decorative lacquered tableware.

A RUSSIAN KITCHEN

A Russian kitchen is traditionally well-stocked with food and a wide range of utensils.

Measuring spoons, cups and a set of scales are essential (when amount of water needs to be accurate, weight is used rather than volume).

A mortar and pestle is excellent for making fruit-flavoured drinks and kisel (a traditional fruit dish), to grind the aromatic oils from the fruit rind.

Saucepans generally should be large with well-fitting lids. Use enamel or stainless steel pans, as marinades and fruits shouldn't be cooked in aluminium or copper.

A rolling pin and pastry brush for glazes are important kitchen tools when making pastry, and at best, one large, flat baking tray for baking pirogi (pies) and buns (make sure it fits your oven).

A sifter for sifting flour and a colander for straining ingredients are essential.

It is important to have a range of sharp knives for paring vegetables and fruits, and for cutting meat. A knife sharpener is also a worthwhile investment if you do have a good selection of knives.

A wooden spoon is a handy tool for mixing batters. A spoon with slits, and tongs, are essential for turning piroshki (small pastries) cooked in oil.

It is useful to have a variety of mixing bowls of different sizes. You need a large bowl for yeast dough as the bowl will fill almost to capacity when the dough has risen.

Since zakuski (appetisers or snacks) are placed on the table, a number of serving platters, bowls, tureens and other dishes are used for serving and presentation. Large pies are generally cut into portions before being served.

Kitchen paper towels and greaseproof paper are also essential. The author recommends that pastries and other foods containing fat or oil, are not wrapped in plastic wrap.

Russian cooks have traditionally cooked with fat or lard. However today Russians, like all of us, are more concerned with weight, diet and health, and lighter vegetable oils have replaced the traditional fats.

In summer, when there is a greater abundance of fresh fruits and vegetables, many people like to make up a good stock of homemade preserves, spiced and pickled vegetables, fruits and mushrooms — for their all year round use. Relishes for traditional meat dishes are made with vegetables or berries. The other ingredients are honey or vinegar — white vinegar is usually used. Most traditional relishes are made from onion, cabbage and cranberry.

French Dressing

Essential Stocks, Sauces and Dressings

STOCKS

The basic stocks used in Russian cooking are made from meat, bones, fish, chicken and mushrooms. These stocks are an essential and integral part of the cooking style, used in soups, sauces and main dishes.

Make stock ahead of time, and store it in the refrigerator or freezer.

MEAT STOCK

2–3 litres water
1 kg shin beef
2 bay leaves
1 teaspoon black peppercorns

Combine water, meat and spices in a large saucepan and bring to the boil. Turn down the heat and simmer for 1½–2 hours or until meat is tender. Remove meat. Strain stock and store.

The meat has to be refrigerated and added to soup at the appropriate time or it can be eaten separately with mustard and vegetables.
Makes 2–3 cups

BONE STOCK

2 large beef bones
2–3 litres water
2 bay leaves

Ask your butcher to chop each bone into 3 or 4 pieces so that the marrow is exposed.

Bring water to the boil in a large saucepan, add beef pieces and bay leaves and simmer 2–2½ hours, or until the bones are hollow. Remove bay leaves and allow stock to cool. This stock has a more delicate flavour than meat stock. It will gelatinise on cooling and liquidise again on heating.

This stock is suitable for potato, barley or vegetable soups.
Makes 2–3 cups

FISH STOCK

500–800 g whole fish, cleaned
2–2.5 litres water
1 onion, peeled
1 parsnip, scraped

Clean fish and remove head, gills and tail. Place whole fish in saucepan of water with onion and parsnip, and boil gently for about 30 minutes. Remove edible fish. Simmer head, tail and vegetables for another 20–30 minutes.

Remove bones from fish fillet. Store fillet for either main course or to add to fish soup. Return bones to stock and simmer for another 20 minutes. Strain well and store in refrigerator.
Makes 2–3 cups

CHICKEN STOCK

1 medium-sized chicken, with giblets
1 onion, peeled and sliced
1½–2 litres water

Place fowl, giblets and onion in a large saucepan and add enough water to cover. Bring to the boil and skin off any scum. Simmer for about 2 hours until meat is tender and easily separated from the bone.

Remove meat and giblets and allow soup to simmer further. Discard skin and separate meat from bone with a small sharp knife. Cut meat into small pieces and either add to the soup again, or serve separately with vegetables. Otherwise, refrigerate and use for other dishes.
Makes 2–3 cups

MUSHROOM STOCK

50 g dried mushrooms
1 litre water

Rinse mushrooms, add to water in a large saucepan and soak for 4–8 hours. Cook in the same water by bringing to the boil, then simmer for about 5–8 minutes or until soft, mixing occasionally.

Remove mushrooms, drain and mince. These may be used in sauces. Strain the stock and store.
Makes 2–3 cups

SAUCES

Sauce is the basic element of many different dishes and is the secret of achieving the right flavour for a particular dish. Many of the sauces are made from the stock (meat, fish and mushroom) or liquid made specially by cooking bones, fish heads and trimmings.

TOMATO SAUCE

15 g butter
1 tablespoon flour
500 mL bone stock (see recipe)
100 g tomato puree
1 small onion, chopped
1 carrot, scraped and grated

Melt butter, add flour and heat until golden brown. Mix in stock and tomato puree, stirring constantly. Bring to the boil, add onion and carrot and simmer for 5 minutes.
Variation:
Fresh or canned mushrooms can be added to the basic sauce; extra spices such as peppercorns and bay leaf, or lemon juice, wine or vinegar for piquancy. Its character can also be altered by adding prunes and raisins to the boiling mixture. Simmer this sauce for 15 minutes then add chopped walnuts.
Makes 2 cups

MUSTARD SAUCE

3 egg yolks
2 teaspoons sugar
1 small teaspoon prepared mustard
2 tablespoons sunflower oil
2 tablespoons vinegar

Beat egg yolks, sugar and mustard together. Add oil gradually while stirring. The mixture will thicken considerably. Dilute with vinegar; only use half initially — the amount necessary will depend on the size of the egg yolks.
Makes ½ cup

MUSHROOM SAUCE (1)

½ cup mushroom stock (see recipe)
2 tablespoons flour
2 onions, peeled and sliced
20 g butter
mushrooms, washed and thinly sliced

Heat the stock and blend a little of it with the flour. Blend thoroughly until smooth: then add to the rest of stock. Boil the mixture gently for 5–10 minutes.

Fry onion in butter to soften (do not brown) and add to stock with the mushrooms. Boil 5–10 minutes.
Makes ½ cup

Variation:

SWEET MUSHROOM SAUCE

300–400 g mushroom sauce (see recipe)
50 g pitted prunes
20 g raisins
100 g tomato puree
sugar to taste

Prepare the mushroom sauce as for (1) then add prunes, raisins, tomato puree and sugar to taste. Boil gently for 10–15 minutes.
Makes 1 cup

DRESSINGS

MAYONNAISE

2 egg yolks
1 teaspoon sugar
1 teaspoon prepared mustard
1 cup sunflower oil
1 tablespoon lemon juice or vinegar

Beat egg yolks, sugar and mustard together. Add oil drop by drop, stirring constantly. The mixture will be very thick — use a little vinegar to dilute it.
Makes ½ cup

MAYONNAISE WITH SOUR CREAM

1 cup mayonnaise (see recipe)
1 cup sour cream
1 tablespoon lemon juice
1 sprig fresh dill, finely chopped

Mix mayonnaise with sour cream and lemon juice and sprinkle with dill.
Makes 1½–2 cups

FRENCH DRESSING

⅔ cup sunflower oil
⅓ cup vinegar or lemon
1 clove garlic, peeled and crushed

Combine oil and vinegar or lemon in a screw-top jar. Add garlic and mix well. Store in the refrigerator, but bring to room temperature before serving.
Makes 1 cup

Mayonnaise
1 Place egg yolks, sugar and mustard in a mixing bowl

2 Beat ingredients together with a whisk to mix well

3 Add oil drop by drop, stirring constantly

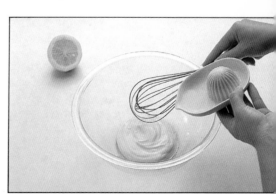

4 Use a little lemon juice or vinegar to obtain desired consistency

Mustard Sauce

APPETISING OPENERS

ZAKUSKI

The zakuski course is a Russian institution, reminiscent of a Swedish smorgasbord or a French cold buffet in that a variety of hot and cold dishes are served. Zakuski (literally 'snacks') consist of salted and pickled foods, cooked eggs, different breads, salads and vegetables. Traditionally these appetisers were served with different kinds of vodka, which was never sipped but taken in one quick swallow, followed by food, then another glass of vodka, and so on.

Zakuski are served on the table using large platters and tureens. Although eaten with a knife and fork, food is usually cut into bite-sized pieces, except for meat and pies.

COLESLAW
SALAT S KAPUSTOI

1 sugarloaf cabbage, shredded
  (see Note)
salt
1 teaspoon sugar
2 tablespoons lemon juice
2 tablespoons sunflower oil

Sprinkle cabbage with salt and rub until crispness is lost. Squeeze and pat dry with paper towelling. Combine sugar, lemon juice and oil in a screw-top jar and shake lightly. Pour over cabbage.
Note: Sugarloaf cabbage is conical-shaped and sweeter tasting than white cabbage.
Serves 4

Variations:

RED CABBAGE SLAW

Substitute whole red cabbage for sugarloaf cabbage.

SAUERKRAUT SLAW

Substitute 500 g sauerkraut. Omit salt. Add dressing to sauerkraut.

CABBAGE AND CELERY SLAW

Substitute 500 g green or white cabbage for sugarloaf. Add 1 stick chopped celery. Add salt and follow method above.

Salted Herring, salmon caviar, Savoury Eggs, Red Cabbage Slaw, rye bread, Radishes with Sour Cream, Dill Tomato, lumpfish caviar, smoked salmon

PICKLED CUCUMBERS
SOLYONYE OGURTSY

1 teaspoon salt
1 cup water
6 Lebanese cucumbers, washed
2 cloves garlic, coarsely chopped
1 sprig fresh dill, finely chopped

Add salt to water in a saucepan and bring brine to the boil.

Place cucumbers in an earthenware or glass container with a lid and pour brine over them. When cool add garlic and dill. Close container and store at room temperature for 2–3 days till cucumbers change colour, then store in refrigerator.

Note: When preparing pickled dishes remember not to use an aluminium pan.

Serves 3

DILL TOMATO
TOMATY

4 large, ripe tomatoes, sliced
1 sprig fresh dill, finely chopped
ground black pepper

Arrange tomato slices on plate. Sprinkle with dill and pepper to serve. Serve with French Dressing (see recipe).

Serves 6

VEAL BRAWN
ZALIVNOE

1 whole breast of veal
2 pigs trotters
1 large onion, peeled
1 large carrot, scraped
water
6 whole peppercorns
3 bay leaves
2 cloves garlic, crushed

Place veal, trotters, onion and carrot into a cast iron pot or large heavy casserole dish. Cover contents with water. Bring to the boil. Remove any scum. Add peppercorns, bay leaves and garlic and simmer for about 3 hours until meat is tender and falling off the bones.

Remove meat and vegetables from stock. Boil stock on high heat until reduced to approximately 1 litre. Set aside to cool.

Remove meat from bone and gristle with a small sharp knife. Discard bone and gristle. Shred meat into small pieces.

Slice carrot into thin rounds. Arrange carrot in concentric circles in a suitable deep mould. Add stock carefully until carrots are half covered. They must not float in the liquid. Chill in refrigerator for approximately 1 hour or until stock is set.

Remainder of stock should now be cool. Strain out bay leaves, peppercorns and garlic. Stir in meat. Mix well. Pour into chilled mould on top of carrots. Refrigerate for at least 4 hours or preferably overnight.

To turn out the mould, run a wet knife around the edge of the meat. Place bottom of mould briefly into hot water. Invert onto a chilled serving dish.

Cut the veal into slices ready for serving. In hot climates it is preferable to keep this dish refrigerated until required.
Serves 8–10

Dill Tomato

SALTED HERRING
SELYODKA

2 salted herrings

GARNISH
2 hard–boiled eggs, finely chopped
1 chopped onion
1 tablespoon capers
sprig fresh dill, finely chopped

Soak herrings in plenty of water, for 3–4 hours.

Clean herrings by cutting off the edge of the belly, head and tail. Remove viscera. Slit skin from head to tail along the backbone. Peel off skin starting at head end and pulling towards the tail end. Remove backbone and ribs.

Place fillets together and cut into bite–sized pieces. Arrange fish on oblong herring plate. Replace head at one end and tail at the other. Both heads should be at the same end of plate.

Arrange garnish so that chopped egg is placed along the sides of herrings. Onion and capers are placed at head and tail ends. Dill is sprinkled lightly over all other garnish.
Serves 8

CORNED BEEF TONGUE
YAZYK

1 corned beef tongue
1 whole turnip, scrubbed
1 large carrot, scrubbed
1 large parsnip, scrubbed
1 large onion, peeled
bay leaf
mayonnaise

Place tongue, vegetables and bay leaf in large saucepan and add water to cover. Boil tongue and vegetables over low heat for 3–3½ hours until tender.

When tongue is ready, remove from saucepan, rinse in cold water and immediately skin.

Remove vegetables and strain cooking liquid.

Place tongue and vegetables in colander. Remove vegetables. Cover tongue with small plate and place approximately 2 kg weight (cans of food will do) on top. Press tongue for approximately 24 hours. Place plate under colander to collect any drips while in refrigerator.

To serve, slice tongue into thin slices. Chop vegetables into julienne pieces, discarding bay leaf and mix well with mayonnaise. Serve in separate dish.
Serves 10–12

GRATED BEETROOT
SVYOKLA

3 medium-sized beetroot, cooked, peeled and grated
4 tablespoons natural yoghurt
½ cup walnuts, finely chopped

Let grated beetroot stand in colander for 10 minutes to drain. Combine beetroot, yoghurt and nuts and mix well.
Serves 4–6

MEAT BALLS IN SAVOURY TOMATO SAUCE
TEFTELI

500 g lean topside mince
1 onion, minced
1 cup soft breadcrumbs
3 cloves garlic, crushed
2 tablespoons flour
2 tablespoons sunflower oil
1 cup beef stock (see recipe)
2 bay leaves
1 cup tomato sauce (see recipe)
1 teaspoon Worcestershire sauce
5 whole black peppercorns
1 small red chilli pepper, finely chopped (see Note)

Combine minced topside and onion with breadcrumbs and garlic and mix well. Roll into small balls of about 30 g each. Roll balls in flour and fry in oil.

Transfer balls to casserole dish. Add stock, bay leaves, tomato sauce, Worcestershire sauce, peppercorns and chilli pepper. Cover with a lid and simmer for 20 minutes. This dish can be served hot or cold.
Note: Wash your hands after finely chopping chilli pepper.
Serves 4–6

EGGPLANT 'CAVIAR'
BAKLAZHANNAYA IKRA

1 large eggplant, halved
2 large, ripe tomatoes
1 tablespoon sunflower oil
2 onions, finely chopped
1 clove garlic, finely chopped
¼ cup water

Grill eggplant halves with flat side down for about 5 minutes or until skin starts to shrink or char. Remove from griller, allow to cool then remove skin.

Soak tomatoes in boiling water for 5 minutes then rinse under a cold running tap. Remove the skins and finely chop tomatoes.

Heat oil in frying pan then slightly sweat onions without browning them.

Chop eggplant into small pieces and add to onion. Stir-fry for about 5 minutes or until eggplant has changed colour. Add garlic and tomato. Cook for 2 minutes.

Add water, stir well and cover. Simmer for about 5–6 minutes until paste consistency. Transfer to serving bowl and refrigerate. When ready, serve caviar with toasted bread fingers, crispbread or crackers.
Serves 4

CAVIAR
IKRA

The famous delicacy we know as caviar is called 'Ikra' in Russia. A variety of caviar is available: not all types are expensive, some are improved by a slice of lemon, can be eaten with rye bread, on toast or biscuits, and are enhanced by an accompaniment of chopped hard-boiled eggs or shallots.

TYPES OF CAVIAR
Black Beluga: Comes from sturgeon and has the largest, finest eggs.
Grey Beluga: Same high grade of sturgeon caviar; distinguished from black by colour alone.
Osetrovaya: Black, smaller than beluga eggs; from a medium-sized sturgeon.
Sevryuga: From the smallest sturgeon; eggs are black and smaller with a more compact consistency; like beluga and osetrovaya, may be sold fresh as malossol (lightly salted) caviar.
Pressed caviar: Usually a combination of osetrovaya and sevryuga eggs.
Saltwater salmon caviar: The roe of salmon caught in the sea; red in colour and relatively inexpensive.
Lumpfish caviar: The roe of lumpfish and whitefish dyed deep black; quite inexpensive.
Freshwater salmon caviar: Eggs of freshwater salmon caught during migration to upstream spawning beds; paler in colour than saltwater salmon roe.

TO SERVE

A selection of caviar, according to taste and budget
1 lemon, thinly sliced

Arrange caviar on a glass or crystal platter which has been chilled and garnish with lemon slices and serve with rye bread.

OPEN SANDWICHES
BUTERBRODY OTKRITIYE

CRAB TOPPING
210 g can crab (Alaskan crab, if available)
1 tablespoon mayonnaise
fresh dill, finely chopped
2 slices rye bread

Drain crab and remove any membranes. Mix well in a bowl with mayonnaise and dill. Spread on fingers of rye bread.

ANCHOVY BUTTER TOPPING

50 g can anchovies
20 g butter, softened
3 slices white bread, halved, no crusts

Drain anchovies and mash with butter until smooth. Spread on triangles of white bread.

CHICKEN TOPPING

butter
6 crispbread
6 breasts chicken, grilled or fried
2 cucumbers, salted and thinly sliced lengthways

Butter crispbreads. Arrange chicken breasts on top of crispbread. Top each piece of chicken with cucumber.

COLD ROAST LAMB OR PORK TOPPING

6 slices roast meat
6 rounds crusty white bread, Vienna-style
1 shallot, finely chopped
3 tablespoons sauerkraut

Arrange roast meat on bread. Mix onion with sauerkraut and spread evenly over meat.

FRIED BREAD SANDWICHES
BUTERBRODY PODZHARENNYE

Fry slices of white bread in butter until crisp and golden. Each side needs 1½ minutes. Drain and serve hot with the topping of your choice (see recipes)

COTTAGE CHEESE TOPPING

6 tablespoons cottage cheese
pepper to taste

Spread cottage cheese over bread and sprinkle with pepper.

SARDINE BUTTER TOPPING

50 g can sardines, drained
20 g butter
fresh dill, finely chopped

Mash sardines with butter, spread evenly on bread and sprinkle with dill.

SAUSAGE TOPPING

3 cooked pork sausages
2 hard-boiled eggs, shelled
1 tablespoon cream
pepper to taste

Place all ingredients in blender. Blend till smooth then spread evenly on fried bread fingers.

Radishes with Sour Cream

SAVOURY EGGS

4 soft–boiled eggs, unpeeled
1 tablespoon mayonnaise
1 small onion, finely chopped
sprig fresh dill, finely chopped

The eggs should have a consistency of hard white with yolk just a little runny. Use a sharp knife to cut egg in half lengthways without damaging the shells.

Carefully remove egg from shells and set shells aside. In a mixing bowl, mash egg pulp, mayonnaise and onion.

Spoon mixture into shells and grill for about 2 minutes to set the mixture a little. Take care not to burn the shells. Sprinkle with dill to serve.
Serves 4

RADISHES WITH SOUR CREAM

REDISKA SO SMETANOI

15–20 small, round radishes, washed
    and thinly sliced
1 hard–boiled egg, chopped
¼ cup sour cream
sprigs fresh dill

Combine radish slices with egg and sour cream and mix well. Arrange on a glass plate and garnish with dill.
Serves 4

SOUPS

Russian soups have traditionally been one of the most basic and economical meals — they are filling, nourishing and popular with everyone. Most soups are made up of five basic ingredients, with many small variations: cabbage, meat (or sometimes fish or dried or salted mushrooms), root vegetables (such as carrots and parsnips), seasoning (such as onion, celery, garlic, dill, pepper, bay leaf) and tart or sour flavouring (such as sour cream, apples, sauerkraut brine).

Traditional Russian soups have not changed much over time. In the dinner menu the term 'first course' (pokhlebka) still means soup. The different kinds are shchi (cabbage soup), borscht (beet soup), rassolnik (cucumber pickle and brine soup), ooha (freshwater fish soup) and solyanka (tart soup which has sauerkraut or pickled cucumbers in it, as well as other savoury ingredients).

The following soups can be stored for 2–3 days in the refrigerator. Ingredients are added to the soup in a definite order so that they are all ready at the same time.

NOODLES COOKED IN BROTH
LAPSHA

1.5 litres bone stock (see recipe)
1 carrot, scraped and diced
1 parsnip, scraped and diced
1 white onion, peeled and finely chopped
40 g butter
150–200 g egg noodles
3 sprigs fresh dill, finely chopped

Bring stock to the boil. Saute carrot, parsnip and onion lightly in butter and add to boiling stock.

Add egg noodles and boil for 15–20 minutes. Before serving garnish soup with dill.
Serves 8

CABBAGE SOUP
SHCHI

1 shredded sugarloaf cabbage
3 carrots, scraped and julienned
1 parsnip, scraped and julienned
2 white onions, peeled and finely chopped
500 g potatoes, peeled and halved (if large)
1.5 litres meat stock (see recipe)
2 tomatoes, skinned
2 sprigs fresh dill, finely chopped

Combine cabbage, carrots, parsnip, onions, potatoes and stock in a saucepan and bring to the boil. Boil 15–20 minutes then add quartered tomatoes and bring to the boil again. Remove from heat and sprinkle with dill to serve.
Serves 6

Royal Doulton Pavanne tableware

Noodles Cooked in Broth

UKRAINIAN BORSCH

BORSCH

½ cup dried lima or broad beans
500 g tomatoes
2 litres meat stock (see recipe)
2 large potatoes, peeled, washed and
    julienned
2 large carrots, scraped
1 large onion, peeled and chopped
1 stalk celery, julienned
2 large beetroot, washed
400–500 g green or white cabbage,
    shredded

GARNISH
sour cream
1 clove fresh garlic, chopped
1 sprig fresh dill, finely chopped

Soak beans overnight. Place tomatoes
in a saucepan of boiling water for 5
minutes. Remove and wash under
running water before removing
skins.

Prepare meat stock according to
recipe. Add potatoes, carrots, onion
and celery to stock, together with
beans and whole beetroot. Bring to
the boil and simmer for 40–50 minutes with the lid on or until vegetables are cooked. Add cabbage and
tomatoes. Cook for 10–15 minutes.

Remove beetroot, grate finely and
return to soup. DO NOT HEAT soup,
but allow to stand for 10 minutes
with closed lid (see *Note*).

Serve in large soup plates. Garnish
with a tablespoon of sour cream, a
little garlic and sprinkle with fresh
dill.

Note: The soup should be a bright red
colour. Heating the beetroot will
cause the colour to change.
Serves 8

FISH SOUP

UKHA

1.5 litres fish stock including fish (see
    recipe)
1 leek, washed and finely chopped
1 stalk celery, finely chopped
3 large potatoes, peeled

Put fish stock in a saucepan and
bring to the boil. Add the leek and
celery and simmer for 10 minutes.

Cut each potato into about 6 pieces
and add to soup. Cook 10–15 minutes
until potato pieces begin to disinte-
grate.
Serves 6

CLASSIC CHICKEN SOUP

KURINYI BULYON

1 litre chicken stock (see recipe)
1 egg, beaten
1 tablespoon milk
½ tablespoon flour

Put chicken stock in a saucepan and
bring to the boil. Whisk egg and milk
in a cup, and add flour. Mix well.

Slowly pour cup mixture into boiling stock, stirring continuously.
Remove from heat and let stand for
10 minutes. Stir gently before serving.
Serves 4

COLD FISH AND VEGETABLE SOUP

BOTVINYA

1 large bunch spinach leaves, washed
    and thick stems removed
1 large bunch sorrel or English-style
    spinach leaves, washed and thick
    stems removed
3 tablespoons grated horseradish
1 teaspoon sugar
1 litre kvas (see recipe)
2 white onions, peeled and chopped
250 g white fish fillets, poached and
    cooled

Place spinach and sorrel leaves in a
saucepan (see note) and cover well
with water. Cook for 10 minutes in
covered saucepan till tender. Drain
vegetables in a colander and discard
water.

Puree or blend the leaves until
smooth. Add horseradish and sugar
then stir in the kvas and chill for 2
hours.

To serve, add onion and fish or,
alternatively, serve the fish separately.
Note: Use a stainless steel or enamel
saucepan, not aluminium.
Serves 4

COLD KVAS SOUP

SUP KHOLODNYI IZ KVASA

400 g sauerkraut, washed and drained
1 large white onion, peeled and sliced
1 sprig fresh dill, finely chopped
1 small green cucumber, thinly sliced
30 g grated horseradish
3 hard–boiled eggs, peeled and
    chopped
1.5 litres kvas (see recipe)
3 tablespoons sour cream

Combine vegetables and eggs in a
mixing bowl then stir in the kvas.
Serve with sour cream.
Serves 6

COLD KVAS SOUP WITH VEGETABLES

OKROSHKA

1 carrot, cooked and grated
2 potatoes, cooked and diced
1 white onion, peeled and chopped
1 turnip, cooked and grated
2 hard–boiled eggs
1 teaspoon mustard
1 litre kvas (see recipe)
1 cucumber, sliced
fresh dill, finely chopped
2 tablespoons sour cream

Combine carrot, potatoes, onion and
turnip in a mixing bowl. Separate egg
yolks from whites. Finely chop
whites. Rub yolks together with mustard and add to vegetables. Stir the
kvas into the mixture then add
cucumber and egg white.

To serve, sprinkle each serving
with dill and add a little sour cream.
Serves 4

Ukrainian Borsch

COLD SORREL SOUP

SUP KHOLODNYI IZ SHCHAVELYA

20 sorrel or English-style spinach
    leaves, washed and stems removed
1 onion, peeled and finely chopped
2 litres water
3–4 hard–boiled eggs, peeled
250 g cucumber, thinly sliced
1 sprig fresh dill, finely chopped
150 g cream

Bring sorrel, onion and water to the boil in a large saucepan and simmer for 10 minutes. Allow to cool.

Separate egg whites from yolks. Chop whites very finely.

To serve, pour sorrel soup into a suitable deep plate. Add egg whites, cucumber slices and the dill. At the last moment combine egg yolks with cream and blend well. Top soup with cream mixture.
Serves 6

HOT SORREL SOUP

RASSOLNIK

20 g butter
1 large onion, peeled and thinly sliced
1 stick celery, chopped
2 pickled cucumbers, sliced
20 sorrel or English-style spinach
    leaves, shredded coarsely
1.5 litres meat stock (see recipe)
1 egg
3 tablespoons sour cream

Melt butter in a large saucepan. Stir–fry onion and celery for about 10 minutes or until soft. (Onions should not brown.) Stir in cucumber and sorrel.

Pour in the beef stock, stir and bring to the boil. Cover with lid and simmer for 15–20 minutes.

Whisk egg lightly in a cup and add a little of the hot soup slowly while whisking. Pour egg mixture into soup, stirring constantly. Remove from heat. DO NOT BOIL EGG MIXTURE.

Place in a large soup tureen and serve with cream if desired.
Serves 8

Hot Sorrel Soup

HEARTY MEAT AND VEGETABLE SOUP

MYASNAYA SOLYANKA

2 large onions, peeled and sliced
20 g butter
2 tablespoons tomato puree
3 cucumbers, salted and sliced
1.5 litres meat stock (see recipe)
500 g meat from stock
1 bay leaf
1 tablespoon capers
6 olives
2 sprigs fresh dill, finely chopped

Saute onion in butter in a large saucepan and add tomato puree. Add the cucumbers and simmer gently for 10 minutes then add stock. Dice meat from stock and add to mixture with bay leaf and capers. Boil gently for approximately 10 minutes.

To serve, place an olive in each plate, pour out soup and sprinkle with dill.
Serves 6

BROTH WITH DUMPLINGS

BULYON S KLOTSKAMI

1.5 litres meat, bone or chicken stock
    (see recipes)
batter for dumplings (see recipes)

Heat stock in a saucepan until nearly boiling then prepare batter for dumplings. Drop batter into boiling stock with a teaspoon. Dumplings will rise to the surface. Cook for 1–2 minutes after they have risen.
Serves 4–6

BATTER FOR DUMPLINGS

FLOUR DUMPLINGS

¼ cup meat stock (see recipe)
1 egg
10 g butter
½ cup flour

Stir stock, egg and butter together. Fold in the flour and beat until smooth.

POTATO DUMPLINGS

3 potatoes, peeled and boiled
2 eggs
1 tablespoon flour

Puree potatoes. Add raw egg yolks and mix thoroughly. Beat egg whites till stiff and fold in mixture. Add flour and beat till smooth.

Batter for Potato Dumplings

1 Beat egg whites until stiff peaks form

2 Fold egg whites through potato mixture

3 Use two teaspoons to form dumpling

SALADS AND VEGETABLE DISHES

SALADS

Traditionally, salads were rarely eaten as whole meals but were served as part of the zakuski course. In the past, salads were not considered an important part of the diet, mainly because of the Russian climate and the need for more substantial food. Times have changed, and salads have become more popular as the Russian diet has changed to suit modern needs.

The 'vinaigrette' salad is the most common salad, usually made with dill cucumbers, potatoes, beetroot and onions. Other popular salad ingredients are beans, cabbage, capsicums and dill.

The weights and measures in this section are only approximate, and can be increased or decreased according to taste and numbers. No two cooks have exactly the same recipe — the end result depends a great deal on what vegetables are in season.

HEALTHY SALAD
SALAT

4 lettuce leaves, shredded
2 tomatoes, diced
1 cucumber, diced
1 white turnip, peeled and grated
2 red apples, diced
1 cup cream
sprig fresh dill, finely chopped

Combine lettuce, tomatoes, cucumber and turnip in a bowl and mix well. Just before serving, add apple and cream and mix all the salad vegetables until immersed in cream. Sprinkle with dill to garnish.
Serves 4

KIDNEY BEAN SALAD
FASOL

250 g kidney beans
1 small onion, chopped
2 tablespoons sunflower oil
1 tablespoon lemon juice

Soak beans overnight in water. Place beans in large saucepan of water and bring to the boil. Boil gently for 1 hour or until tender then drain and allow to cool.

Combine beans, onion, oil and lemon juice in a bowl and mix well. This salad can also be made with haricot beans or broad beans.
Serves 4

Potato Salad, Kidney Bean Salad, Cucumber Salad, lumpfish roe, Healthy Salad, Pickled Mushrooms

Accoutrement Mosman for tableware

Cucumber Salad

1 Score cucumber lightly with a fork

2 Slice thinly and serve

TOMATO AND CUCUMBER SALAD
POMIDORY I OGURTSY

5-6 tomatoes, washed and sliced
2-3 cucumbers, washed and sliced
2 tablespoons sunflower oil
3 tablespoons vinegar
sprig fresh dill, finely chopped

Arrange tomatoes and cucumbers in a serving bowl. Just before serving mix oil and vinegar together in a screw-top jar and pour over salad. Sprinkle with dill to garnish.

Variation:

TOMATO, CUCUMBER AND ONION SALAD

Add 2 small white onions peeled and sliced into rings, to tomato and cucumber before serving.
Serves 6

CUCUMBER SALAD
OGURTSY

3 cucumbers
1 sprig fresh dill, finely chopped
¼ cup sour cream

Wash cucumbers and score skin by running a fork down the length of the skin to make grooves through the skin to the level of the flesh. Do this until the cucumber skin is covered by grooves. This step is important to soften the skin of large or old cucumbers.

Thinly slice cucumber and place in a mixing bowl with the dill. Pour over sour cream, mix well and arrange in a salad bowl.
Serves 6

POTATO SALAD
KARTOFELNYI SALAT

5 potatoes, boiled, peeled and diced
½ cup chopped onion
2 tablespoons sunflower oil
¼ cup vinegar
1 sprig fresh dill, finely chopped

Combine potatoes and onion in a large mixing bowl. To make dressing, shake the oil and vinegar in a screw-top jar. Pour over potatoes and onion. Add dill, toss salad well and place in serving bowl.

This salad is usually eaten with hot or cold veal, pork or fish.
Serves 4

CHICKEN SALAD
SALAT OLIVIER

400-500 g chicken breasts
1 large white onion, peeled and
*   quartered*
100-150 g pickled cucumbers
4 boiled potatoes, peeled and sliced
3 hard-boiled eggs, peeled and sliced
½ cup sour cream
½ cup mayonnaise (see recipe)

GARNISH
1 tablespoon capers
6 green olives
1 tomato, sliced
lettuce leaves

Place chicken and onion in a saucepan, cover with water and bring to the boil. Cover with a lid and simmer for 10 minutes.

Remove chicken from pan. Discard chicken skin, onion and cooking water. Cut the breasts into small pieces.

Mix chicken, cucumbers, potatoes and eggs in a large bowl. To make dressing beat cream and mayonnaise together. Divide into two equal portions and add one half to the salad mixture, stirring well.

The traditional Russian way of serving this salad is in the shape of a pyramid. Arrange the rest of dressing around the edge of the dish and garnish with capers, olives, tomato and lettuce.
Serves 6–8

PICKLED MUSHROOMS
MARINOVANNYE GRIBY

1 cup vinegar
2 cloves
3 black peppercorns
1 bay leaf
2 teaspoons salt
2 cloves garlic, peeled and crushed
6 tablespoons water
500-600 g button mushrooms,
*   washed*
1 tablespoon oil

Place vinegar, cloves, peppercorns, bay leaf, salt, garlic and water in a large saucepan and bring to the boil. Add mushrooms and simmer for 10–15 minutes, stirring occasionally. Cool to room temperature.

Remove garlic from marinade. Pour mushrooms and liquid into a glass or earthenware jar. Slowly pour oil or hot wax over the back of a spoon on top of contents to form a seal. Screw lid on securely. Store in refrigerator for about 1 week before serving.
Serves 6–8

RUSSIAN VINAIGRETTE
VINAIGRETTE

2 large or 4 small beetroot, boiled,
*   peeled and diced*
1 large carrot, scraped, boiled and
*   diced*
400 g potatoes, peeled, boiled and
*   diced*
1 white onion, peeled and diced
1 cucumber, peeled and diced
3 tomatoes, peeled, seeded and finely
*   chopped*
440 g can baked beans in tomato
*   sauce*
1 cup sour cream or natural yoghurt

Combine all vegetables in a mixing
bowl, add the baked beans in sauce,
and mix well. Fold in sour cream
gently but thoroughly so that salad is
well mixed. The salad should be red
in colour.

Note: Vinaigrette is one of the most
popular Russian salads and there are
many variations according to taste
and what's in season.
Serves 6–8

VEGETABLE DISHES

A much greater variety of fresh
vegetables is available in northern
Russia today than in the past. In the
Georgian south the warm climate is
good for growing and the variety has
always been available.

Potatoes, onions, red cabbage,
tomatoes, capsicums, marrow,
cauliflower, pumpkin and eggplant,
are just a few of the vegetables used
in traditional Russian vegetable
dishes.

Stuffed vegetables with a variety of
meat and other fillings are popular.
These dishes are also economical as
only a small amount of meat is
needed.

The recipes in this section can all
be adapted to suit your tastes. Other
vegetables in season can be used to
complement their wholesome
flavours and earthy colours.

Royal Doulton Platinum Concord plates

STUFFED GREEN CAPSICUMS (PEPPERS)
FARSHIROVANNYI PERETS

8 medium–sized green capsicums
4 medium–sized tomatoes
2 tablespoons sour cream

STUFFING
20 g butter
500 g raw minced topside steak
1 onion, peeled and chopped
½ cup long grain rice, cooked
1 carrot, scraped and julienned

To make stuffing, heat butter in a
pan and stir-fry mince, onion, rice
and carrot until meat is cooked
(about 20 minutes). Add a little water
to mixture if necessary and simmer
another 5–10 minutes.

Tomato, Cucumber and
Onion Salad, Stuffed Green
Capsicums, Potato Matchsticks

Cut top off capsicums carefully and
scoop out sides. Spoon prepared
stuffing into capsicums and place in a
greased casserole dish.

Immerse tomatoes in hot water for
about 10 minutes then hold under
running cold water. Remove tomato
skins and place tomatoes in casserole
dish. Break the tomatoes with a fork
and spoon pulp over the peppers.
Bake in a moderate oven of 180°C
(350°F) covered, for about 1 hour.

To serve, add sour cream to the
sauce and reheat.
Serves 4–8

FRIED POTATO WITH EGGS

ZHARENNYI KARTOFEL (1)

40 g butter
1 kg potatoes, peeled and thinly sliced
3 eggs
1 cup milk

Heat butter in a pan and fry potato slices until the edges become crisp.

Whisk eggs and milk together in a bowl. Pour mixture over fried potatoes, simmer gently for about 10 minutes and then serve.

Serves 4–6

FRIED POTATO WITH ONION

ZHARENNYI KARTOFEL (2)

40 g butter
4 large onions, peeled and finely chopped
1 kg potatoes, peeled and thinly sliced

Heat butter in a large frypan and stir–fry onions until soft. Add potatoes and fry gently so as not to break up slices. Potatoes should be served crisp at the edges and soft in the middle.

Serves 4–6

POTATO PUDDING

KARTOFELNAYA ZAPEKANKA

1 kg potatoes, peeled and grated
2 eggs
2 onions, sliced
40 g butter

Preheat oven to 200°C (400°F). Combine potatoes, eggs, onions and butter in a greased medium–sized casserole dish. Bake uncovered for about 25–30 minutes.

To serve, invert pudding from casserole dish to serving plate. Cut into wedges or squares.

Serves 4

POTATOES STEWED IN SOUR CREAM

KARTOFEL SO SMETANOI

40 g butter
1 kg potatoes, peeled and cut into chunks
250 g sour cream
1 teaspoon flour
1 sprig fresh dill, finely chopped

Heat butter in a casserole dish and stir–fry potato pieces. Blend sour cream with flour and pour over potatoes. Simmer, covered for 20–30 minutes until tender. Sprinkle with dill before serving.

Serves 6–8

POTATO MATCHSTICKS OR FRENCH FRIES

ZHARENNYI KARTOFEL

sunflower oil
4 large potatoes, peeled and cut into matchsticks

Pour enough oil into pan for deep frying. While oil is heating, immerse matchsticks into iced water for a few minutes and drain on paper towelling.

When oil is hot, place basket or strainer full of matchsticks into oil for about 15 seconds. The potatoes will be soft and pale. Remove from oil, and drain on paper towelling.

To serve, reheat the oil, place matchsticks in oil as before, for another 15 seconds, until golden brown. Serve immediately.

Serves 4–6

POTATO PATTIES

KARTOFELNYE KOTLETY

1 kg potatoes
20 g butter
2 eggs, beaten
2–3 tablespoons flour
½ cup breadcrumbs
1 cup mushroom stock, including mushrooms (see recipe)
1 tablespoon sour cream

Peel potatoes and boil in water for 20 minutes or until soft. Drain well in a colander. Mash potatoes with half the butter and most of the egg until thoroughly blended. If mixture is too liquid to hold its shape add a little flour. Beat in well.

Place potato dough on a floured board and work it into a thick rectangle. Roll out into a piece about 25–30 cm thick. Cut into rounds. Add a few mushrooms to each, fold over to form a crescent and press edge together. Brush with remainder of egg and coat with breadcrumbs.

Melt rest of butter in a pan and fry patties carefully on high heat. Add about half the patties only at any one time, to avoid burning. Brown patties on each side, 3–5 minutes, turning carefully with a flat knife. When cooked, remove from pan, cover with paper towelling to soak up excess fat, and place in a serving dish. Add mushroom stock to sour cream and blend well. Serve sauce separately in a sauce boat.

Serves 6–8

Potato Patties

1 Place spoonful of filling on blanched cabbage leaf as shown

2 Fold in ends

3 Roll to form a firm parcel

CABBAGE ROLLS
GOLUBTSY

1 large cabbage

STUFFING
2 cups water
2 tablespoons uncooked long grain rice
1 white onion, peeled and finely chopped
500 g raw minced topside

SAUCE
2 carrots, scraped and grated
1 onion, peeled and chopped
3 tablespoons tomato puree
1 cup water or meat or bone stock (see recipes)

Remove the outer damaged cabbage leaves and discard. Fill a large container with boiling water. Carefully separate cabbage leaves one by one and immerse in boiling water. When inner leaves become difficult to separate, immerse whole head in water, then remove each leaf until the leaf becomes too small. Allow leaves to soak in boiling water for about 10 minutes until leaves are no longer crisp or pliable.

Meanwhile, for the stuffing, place water in a saucepan and bring to the boil. Add rice and boil uncovered for about 12 minutes. Drain and set aside.

Combine onion and mince, add rice and mix until well blended.

Drain cabbage leaves. Place one teaspoon stuffing in each leaf and wrap into a tight parcel, tucking in the ends. Place parcels in a large casserole dish, stacking if necessary.

To make sauce, combine carrot, onion, tomato puree and water or stock and pour over parcels in casserole dish.

Cook covered in a moderate oven of 180°C (350°F), for about 45 minutes. Check fluid levels. If necessary, add a little more water and cook uncovered for 20 minutes more or until soft and meat is cooked. Serve parcels with sauce.
Serves 6

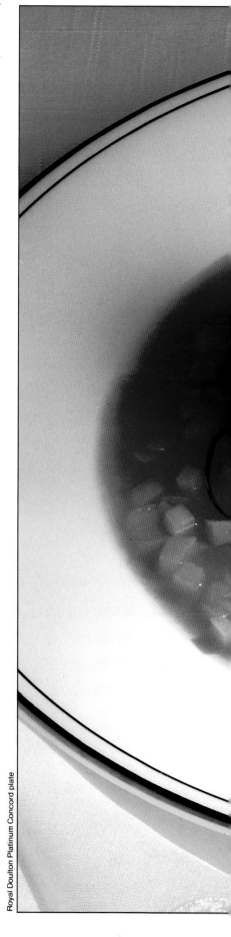

Royal Doulton Platinum Concord plate

Cabbage Rolls

POTATOES STUFFED WITH MEAT

KARTOFEL S MYASOM

8 large potatoes, brown-skinned and regular in shape
40 g butter
500–600 g tomatoes, washed
2 tablespoons sour cream

STUFFING
1 onion, peeled and chopped
40 g butter
500 g raw minced topside steak

To prepare stuffing, stir–fry onion in butter but do not brown. Add mince and fry for about 20 minutes, stirring occasionally.

Peel potatoes and boil in water for 5 minutes. Cut off a flat top, scoop out centre and set aside.

Spoon prepared stuffing into potatoes, and replace tops. Pre-heat oven to 180°C (350°F). Place stuffed potatoes and butter in a greased casserole dish and bake for about 30 minutes.

Add whole tomatoes to casserole and bake for further 20–30 minutes until potatoes are soft. Place potatoes and tomatoes in a serving dish.

To serve, heat pan juices and stir in sour cream. Pour sauce over potatoes and tomatoes.
Serves 4

BUTTERED CAULIFLOWER

TSVETNAYA KAPUSTA

1 small head cauliflower, washed
90 g butter
1 cup dry breadcrumbs

Place cauliflower in saucepan green stalks down, with enough water to cover stalks. Boil gently for 20 minutes then drain.

Melt butter in a small frypan. Add breadcrumbs and mix well. Pour over cauliflower just before serving.
Serves 4

RED CABBAGE WITH SOUR CREAM

KRASNAYA KAPUSTA SO SMETANOI

1 tablespoon sunflower oil
1 red cabbage, shredded
1 onion, peeled and chopped
1 clove garlic, peeled and chopped
1 tablespoon tomato puree
1 tablespoon freshly squeezed lemon
    juice
2 tablespoons sour cream

Heat oil in a large frypan or casserole dish, add cabbage, onion and garlic and stir–fry. When the cabbage has wilted, add tomato puree and lemon juice. Cover and simmer for approximately 10 minutes or until soft. Remove from heat. Stir in sour cream immediately before serving. This dish goes well with meat rissoles.
Serves 6–8

Variation:

RED CABBAGE WITH APPLE PUREE

KRASNAYA KAPUSTA S YABLOKOM

*100 g can apple puree or freshly
    stewed apple (puree consistency)*

Heat oil and stir–fry cabbage, onion and garlic as above. Add pureed apple and lemon juice. Simmer for approximately 10 minutes until soft. Serve with pork or veal.
Serves 6–8

STUFFED ONIONS

FARSHIROVANNYI LUK

4 large onions, peeled
2 tablespoons finely chopped
    mushrooms
40 g butter
2 tablespoons dry breadcrumbs
½ cup water

Cut off tops of onions. Scoop out the centres carefully and put the scooped–out pulp to one side. Stuff onions with mushrooms and arrange in a greased casserole dish. Mix butter with breadcrumbs and sprinkle onions with mixture. Pre-heat oven to 180°C (350°F). Cover casserole dish and bake for about 1 hour, then add water and simmer for 10 minutes more.
Serves 4

STUFFED MARROW

FARSHIROVANNYE KABACHKI

1 large marrow

STUFFING
40 g butter
300 g meat (beef, pork or lamb)
2 tablespoons cooked long grain rice
2 tablespoons finely chopped
    mushrooms
1 peeled, chopped onion

To make stuffing, heat butter in a pan and stir–fry meat, rice, mushrooms and onion until meat is cooked.

Cut end of marrow, scoop out the seeds and spoon in prepared stuffing. Pre-heat oven to 180°C (350°F). Place marrow on greased casserole dish, cover and cook for 40–50 minutes.

To serve, slice in pieces about 2 cm across.
Serves 4

EGGPLANT STUFFED WITH MEAT

BAKLAZHANY S MYASOM

4 medium–sized eggplants

STUFFING
500 g raw minced topside steak
1 onion, peeled and chopped
1 egg
1 tablespoon soft breadcrumbs
sour cream

Remove the end of each eggplant and scoop out the middle with a spoon. To make stuffing mix mince, onion, egg and breadcrumbs thoroughly. Spoon mixture into eggplants. Pre-heat oven to 180°C (350°F). Place eggplants on a greased flat tray and bake for 1 hour or until ready. Five minutes before serving, pour sour cream over the stuffing.
Serves 4

Mikasa cutlery Wedgwood Chester plate

Stuffed Marrow and
Red Cabbage with Sour Cream

FRIED EGGPLANT
BAKLAZHANY ZHARENNYE

4 small to medium-sized eggplants
2 cups hot water
2 tablespoons flour
40 g butter
3 tablespoons sunflower oil

Slice eggplants lengthways, about 1 cm thick. Immerse in hot water so that flesh does not brown, and drain well.

Coat eggplant slices with flour. Heat butter and oil in frypan and fry each slice until golden.
Serves 4

PICKLED CAULIFLOWER
KISLAYA TSVETNAYA KAPUSTA

1 large cauliflower

PICKLING MIXTURE
3 cups water
1 tablespoon salt
1 cup vinegar
1 cup sugar
10 peppercorns
2 cloves
3 bay leaves

To make pickling mixture, combine all ingredients except for cauliflower in a large saucepan, bring to the boil and cook, stirring continuously until sugar dissolves. Set mixture aside to cool.

Break cauliflower up into flowerettes. Wash well, drain then blanch by placing in a saucepan of boiling water for 2 minutes. Drain and cool.

Place cauliflower in suitable glass or earthenware container and pour pickling mixture over it. Seal container and store in a cool place. It should be ready to eat in 2-3 days.
Serves 6-8

Variation:

PICKLED PUMPKIN

2 kg pumpkin, peeled and diced
pickling mixture (see recipe)

Blanche the pumpkin and cover with pickling mixture as above.

Left to right: Pickled Cauliflower, Pickled Pumpkin

MEAT

Russians eat a variety of meats, including beef and lamb, poultry (chicken, duck, and goose) and game (goat, deer and hare or rabbit). There are three types of main meat courses: meat which is boiled in one large piece for making soups and gruels (or porridges) then served cold as a main course after the zakuski or appetisers; dishes made from offal combined with kasha (grains and groats) in a casserole; and a whole or part of a fowl or any large piece of meat, roasted in the oven. Meat dishes also include a range of cutlets, meat balls and meat loaves.

The meat course can be served with the kasha the meat was cooked in and mushrooms and root vegetables, either boiled, steamed or baked. Meat dishes can be accompanied by sauerkraut, pickled apples and various preserves.

Lamb is traditionally associated mainly with the southern and central Asian parts of the USSR, while pork and poultry feature more in northern cooking. Butchering methods vary from region to region, so recipes tend to state the type of meat required rather than a specific cut.

Meat dishes are often served with rice or garnished with vegetables. A variety of fresh vegetables can be used to complement the more traditional root vegetables.

Baked Fillet of Beef

BAKED FILLET OF BEEF

FILE

4 pieces eye fillet
40 g butter
3 onions, peeled and sliced
200 g mushrooms
2 hard-boiled eggs, chopped
½ cup tomato puree mixed with
3 tablespoons red wine
flaky pastry (see recipe)
1 beaten egg

Fry each piece of meat in butter until brown on both sides. Fry onions until brown. Add mushrooms and fry until ready.

Place onion, mushroom on top of each piece of meat. Top with hard-boiled eggs. Pour tomato puree mixture over.

Roll and divide pastry into 4 flat pieces. Cover each piece of meat with pastry. Brush with beaten egg. Place on a flat greased oven tray and bake in a hot oven, 220°C (425°F), for approximately 20 minutes.
Serves 4

BEEF STEW WITH QUINCE

TUSHENOE MYASO S AIVOI

500 g round or topside steak
1 onion, peeled and sliced
40 g butter
1 cup water
4 quinces, peeled, cored and cut into wedges
1 sprig fresh dill, finely chopped

Cut meat into small bite-sized pieces. Brown meat and onion in butter in a casserole dish. Add water and simmer for about 1 hour. Add quinces to casserole and cook until tender. Sprinkle dill over stew before serving.
Serves 4

BEEF STEWED IN KVAS

TUSHENOE MYASO V KVASE

500 g brisket or round steak
4 potatoes, peeled
1 carrot, scraped
1 turnip, peeled
1 onion, peeled and sliced
50 g butter
1 tablespoon flour
1 litre kvas (see recipe)

Cut meat and vegetables into bite-sized pieces. Arrange in a casserole dish in layers of meat and vegetables ending with meat. Melt butter in a pan, add flour and stir until brown. Add to casserole.

Pour kvas over casserole and simmer slowly until kvas has evaporated. If meat is not tender at this stage, add 1 cup water and simmer until it has boiled away.

Variation:

WITH TOMATO PUREE

½ cup tomato puree
½ cup soft breadcrumbs

Add tomato puree to layers of meat and vegetables. Melt butter and mix with breadcrumbs (instead of flour) and add to casserole. Proceed with recipe as above.

STEAK TARTARE
BIFSHTEKS PO-TATARSKI

2 teaspoons French Dressing (see
  recipe)
200–300 g piece rib fillet, minced
1 egg yolk
1 anchovy fillet

Add dressing to mince and mix well.
Shape into a patty, place on serving
plate and flatten with a fork. Make a
well in the middle and place in
refrigerator for 10–20 minutes.

To serve, put egg yolk into the well
and garnish with anchovy.
Serves 1

LIVER PATE
PASHTET

2 tablespoons sunflower oil
500–800 g beef liver, cut into pieces
20 g butter
2 onions, peeled and diced
2 carrots, scraped and chopped
1 bay leaf
¼ teaspoon ground black pepper
1 pinch nutmeg
60 g butter
4 hard-boiled eggs, peeled and halved,
  to garnish

Heat oil in a pan and fry liver, stirring
constantly until cooked. Scrape liver
into a mixing bowl. In the same pan,
add 20 g butter and cook onions and
carrots until soft. Add bay leaf and
add a little water if necessary, to
ensure vegetables are soft and to use
pan juices. When cooked, remove bay
leaf, add vegetables to liver, and
mince twice.

Add pepper and nutmeg to remaining butter and mix well. Add slowly
to liver mixture, beating continuously
until pureed. Either form a loaf shape
or place in a mould, smoothing over
the surface. Refrigerate for at least 8
hours or preferably overnight.

To serve, unmould by running a
knife around the edge of the mould
and invert onto a serving plate. Garnish by placing egg halves around the
plate.
Serves 6–8

RUSSIAN MEAT BALLS
KOTLETY

3 slices thick stale bread
1 kg minced beef
1 onion, peeled and chopped
2 eggs
1 cup dry breadcrumbs
½ cup sunflower oil
Sauce (see recipe)

Soak bread in water and squeeze out
excess liquid. Add meat, onion and
eggs and mix well.

Roll mixture into balls about
20–30 g in size. Coat in breadcrumbs.
Fry gently in oil for 10–15 minutes.
Add prepared sauce and simmer for
10 minutes.
Serves 4–6

SAUCE FOR RUSSIAN MEAT BALLS

(1)
2 tablespoons sour cream

Remove fried meat balls from pan.
Add sour cream to fat in pan with a
little water. Boil vigorously until
water evaporates. Return meatballs
to pan and simmer in sauce for 10
minutes.

(2)
½ cup tomato puree
1 clove garlic, crushed
1 cup meat stock (see recipe)

Combine all ingredients in a saucepan and bring to the boil. Pour over
meat balls and simmer until
reduced by half.

(3)
1 cup mushroom stock, including
  mushrooms (see recipe)
2 tablespoons sour cream

Combine all ingredients in a saucepan and bring to the boil. Pour over
meat balls and simmer until
reduced by half.

(4)
10 pitted prunes
1 clove
bay leaf
½ teaspoon black peppercorns
3 tablespoons sour cream

When meat balls are cooked, place
them in a saucepan with prunes,
clove, bay leaf and peppercorns.
Cover with water and bring to the
boil. Simmer gently for 10 minutes,
add sour cream to the sauce and
mix in well, before serving.

BRAISED BEEF WITH SOUR CREAM
BEF STROGANOFF

1 kg rump steak
100 g butter
4 onions, peeled and sliced
500 g mushrooms, chopped
2 tablespoons flour
2 cups sour cream
2½ teaspoons mustard powder
2 teaspoons sugar
1 teaspoon salt
1 tablespoon water

Flatten steak pieces with a mallet,
then cut into thin strips about 5–6
cm long. Heat butter in a frypan and
brown the onion. Add meat and
mushrooms, stirring constantly for
5–6 minutes until meat is cooked.
Sprinkle flour over meat, stir–fry for
another 2–3 minutes. Stir in sour
cream. Turn off heat and let stand.

Mix mustard powder, sugar and
salt in a small dish. Slowly add 1–2
teaspoons boiling water to form a
thick paste, stirring constantly. Add a
little more water if necessary and
allow to stand for 15 minutes (See
Note).

To serve, add paste to contents of
frypan and heat. Turn out mixture
into a heated serving dish and serve
with either potato matchsticks or
fried potato slices (see recipes).
Note: Allowing meat to stand produces a melding of flavours.
Serves 4–6

Braised Beef with Sour
Cream, Potato Matchsticks

BOILED BEEF WITH HORSERADISH SAUCE
VARYONAYA GOVYADINA S KHRENOM

1 kg shin beef or brisket
2 small hot red chillies
1 teaspoon whole black peppercorns
6 potatoes, peeled
2 carrots, scraped
1 turnip, peeled
1 parsnip, scraped
50 g grated horseradish
2 tablespoons sour cream

Place meat in a saucepan with enough water to cover. Add chillies and peppercorns and bring to the boil. Cover and simmer for 2 hours.

Halve potatoes, carrots, turnip and parsnip. Add to meat and cook for about 30 minutes until tender.

Remove meat and vegetables from stock. Slice meat and garnish with vegetables.

To serve add horseradish to sour cream with a little stock and pour over individual servings of meat.
Serves 4–6

SOUTHERN LAMB STEW
TUSHENAYA BARANINA PO-YUZHNOMU

1 kg lamb pieces
1 large onion, peeled and sliced
2 tablespoons sunflower oil
3 potatoes, peeled and quartered
1 turnip, peeled and halved
2 carrots, peeled and chopped
1 cup water
1 tablespoon flour
2–3 cloves garlic, peeled and crushed

Brown lamb pieces and onion in oil. Put meat, oil and vegetables into a casserole dish. Add water, sprinkle top with flour and add garlic. Simmer for 2 hours with the lid on. Remove lid, turn up heat and boil to reduce fluid by half.
Serves 4–6

LAMB PILAU
PLOV

40 g butter
500 g tender lamb pieces
2 onions, peeled and finely chopped
2 pomegranates, peeled
1 cup water
40 g melted butter
4 cups cooked rice

Heat butter in a pan and fry meat. Add onions and brown. Remove pomegranate segments, taking care to exclude all fibrous segment–dividing tissue. Add pulp to meat, cover with water and simmer for 10 minutes or until tender.

To serve, add melted butter to rice, mix and serve on meat.
Serves 4

MADEIRA LAMB KIDNEYS
POCHKI V MADERE

500 g lamb kidneys
2 cups water with
1 teaspoon salt
40 g butter
300 g fresh mushrooms, chopped
1 tablespoon flour
½ cup Madeira
1 cup meat stock (see recipe)
small potatoes
20 g butter

Clean and split kidneys lengthways. Soak in salted water for 30 minutes. Drain and slice thinly.

Heat 40 g butter in a pan and add mushrooms and kidneys. Sprinkle flour over mixture and stir–fry for 2 minutes. Stir in Madeira and meat stock. Boil vigorously for 3–4 minutes until sauce is reduced by half.

Place potatoes in saucepan of water and bring to the boil. Boil gently until cooked. Pour off water, add remaining butter, and serve hot with meat dish.
Serves 4

SHASHLIK WITH POMEGRANATE JUICE
SHASHLYK S GRANATOVYM SOKOM

1 kg lamb pieces
1 large onion, peeled and sliced into rings
1 tablespoon vinegar
ground pepper

TO SERVE
4 cups cooked white rice
4 tomatoes
½ lemon
pomegranate juice or sour plum juice (see recipe)

Cut meat into small pieces suitable for skewering. Place meat, onion, vinegar and pepper in a container with a lid. Cover and set aside to marinate for 2–3 hours.

Drain meat and thread onto skewers alternating with onion. Grill or cook on a spit for 15 minutes turning frequently.

To serve, place skewer on a bed of rice and garnish with wedges of tomato and thin slices of lemon. Pomegranate juice is passed around separately.
Serves 4

POMEGRANATE JUICE

200 mL pomegranate juice or 4–6 pomegranates
100 g sugar
200 mL water

To squeeze juice from pomegranates, choose ripe fruit which are well coloured. Peel skin and remove pulp segments. Place pulp in a colander resting in a deep dish. Grind with a mortar or the back of a large spoon. The juice will drain through the colander. Combine juice, sugar and water and store in a cool place.
Serves 4

Boiled Beef with Horseradish Sauce

Garlic Breast of Veal

1 Place slivers of garlic into pockets between ribs

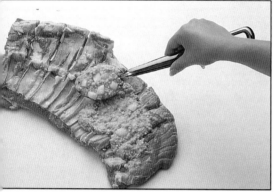

2 Spread stuffing over inside of breast as shown

3 Roll up veal and secure firmly with a string

GARLIC BREAST OF VEAL

TELYACHYA GRUD

1 breast of veal
salt
1 clove garlic, peeled

STUFFING
2 cups buckwheat kasha (see recipe) or cooked white rice
1 onion, peeled and chopped
2 eggs
40 g butter

Get your butcher to chop veal ribs from the inside (not right through meat). Rub breast with salt and then garlic. Chop the garlic into slivers. With a sharp knife make pockets between the ribs and insert garlic.

Mix stuffing ingredients together and cover inside breast with stuffing. Roll up veal and secure with string. Pre-heat oven to 180°C (350°F).

Place veal on a greased baking tray and bake for 1–1½ hours or until done. Timing will depend on size of breast.

To serve, cut portions crossways between ribs and pour pan juices over individual serves.
Serves 4–6

Variation:

ROLLED VEAL SHOULDER

Get the butcher to bone the shoulder for you. Follow recipe above, using shoulder instead of breast.
Serves 4–6

PIGS TROTTERS

SVINNYE NOZHKI

4 pigs trotters
salt and pepper
1 bay leaf

Wash trotters well. Pluck or singe any hairs and place in a saucepan with salt, pepper, bay leaf and water to cover. Bring to the boil and simmer 3–4 hours until meat comes off the bone. Traditionally served with potatoes (see recipes).
Serves 4

PORK WITH APPLE

SVININA C YABLOKAMI

1 kg pork loin
4 tart Granny Smith apples, peeled, cored and chopped
2 cups bone or meat stock (see recipes)

Cut loin into 4 pieces. Put the apple on the meat and wrap like an envelope so that all flaps are folded over. Place in saucepan with folds facing downwards. Pour stock over parcels. Bring to the boil and simmer for about 45 minutes.
Serves 4–6

BARBECUE SUCKING PIG

POROSYONOK

1 small sucking pig
3 tablespoons salt
3 tablespoons sunflower oil
1 apple

Get the butcher to remove the pig's head for you. Slit the body open lengthways to chop pelvic bone and vertebrae so that it can be flattened out. Rub skin and cavities with salt. Brush the skin with oil. Attach head and body to a spit. Place an apple or quantity of foil in the pig's mouth to keep it open. Place foil caps on the ears and nose to prevent burning.

Roast pig for 1½–2 hours, basting continually or until the skin is crisp. Timing will depend on size of the pig. Insert fork into the meat. If cooked the liquid should run clear. About 10 minutes before pig is done remove ear and nose caps and baste with oil.

The traditional Russian way of serving sucking pig is with buckwheat kasha (see recipe).
Serves a crowd

Roast Goose with Apple

HAM AND SAUERKRAUT
SOLYANKA

20 g butter
1 kg sauerkraut
1 onion, peeled and chopped
½ teaspoon black peppercorns
1 bay leaf
500 g cooked ham, chopped
200 g garlic sausage, chopped

Heat butter in a pan and fry sauerkraut and onion, stirring constantly on low heat for about 15 minutes or until wilted and soft. Add peppercorns, bayleaf and meat and stir well. Cover and allow to cook in pan juices for 10 minutes. If mixture is too dry, add a half cup of water. Remove peppercorns and bay leaf before serving.
Serves 4

POULTRY

Various kinds of poultry are used in Russian cooking as the versatile basis of many different dishes. Roast goose is a particular favourite and Chicken Kiev has been exported around the world. In rural areas wild game birds are often roasted, while in the Ukraine, poultry is reserved for holiday and festival food.

ROAST GOOSE WITH APPLE
GUS ZHARENNYI S YABLOKAMI

1 medium–sized goose, cleaned
1 kg Granny Smith apples, peeled, cored and quartered
1 cup water

Prepare goose by washing well inside and out under running water. Stuff goose with apple and place in a roasting pan. Add about a cup of water to the pan and bake for about 2 hours at 180°C (350°F). This dish is traditionally served with buckwheat kasha (see recipe).
Serves 6

CHICKEN KIEV

KOTLETY PO-KIEVSKI

4 large chicken breasts
200 g butter
1 egg yolk
½ cup flour
2 beaten eggs
dry breadcrumbs
extra butter for frying

Wash and dry breasts, removing any connective tissue or skin. Place smooth side on cutting board and pound to flatten to about 5 mm thickness.

Combine butter with yolk of 1 egg and divide into 4 equal parts. Roll into sausage shapes 7–8 cm long. Cover each with greaseproof paper and chill until the pieces are very hard.

Wrap the breasts around each piece of butter creating 4 parcels. Dip in flour, one at a time. Shake off excess flour and pat flat in the palm of the hand. Dip in beaten eggs and roll in breadcrumbs. Refrigerate for a few hours. Deep–fry in butter until golden brown.

Note: Traditionally Chicken Kiev is served with buckwheat kasha (see recipe) and peas served in small pastry shells. DO NOT REHEAT this dish or keep warm for periods of time, as the butter will melt.

Serves 4

ROASTED WOODCOCK OR QUAIL

VALDSHNEP, PEREPEL ZHARENYI

2 tablespoons sunflower oil
2 woodcock or 4 quail, cleaned and dressed
2 tablespoons water

Heat oil in a casserole dish. Add birds and brown, turning so that skin is golden brown.

Add water, close lid tightly and bake in a moderate oven 180°C (350°F) (woodcock 20–25 minutes, quail 15–20 minutes) until meat is falling off the bone.

Serve meat with pan juices and vegetables.

Serves 4

Chicken Kiev

Wedgwood Silver Ermine plate

Chicken Kiev

1 Pound chicken breast to flatten

2 Place butter on breast and wrap to form a parcel

3 Dip in flour, egg and breadcrumbs before deep-frying

DEER OR WILD GOAT

OLENINA ILI DIKAYA KOZLYATINA

1½–2 kg deer or wild goat meat

MARINADE
4–5 cups water
100 mL vinegar
5–6 bay leaves
1 tablespoon black peppercorns

SAUCE
100 g butter
100 g flour
2 cups strong stock (use pan juices from stewing supplemented by beef stock if necessary)
1 cup berry jam (cranberry, redcurrant)

Cut meat into joints and pieces small enough to be marinated.

Place marinade ingredients in a saucepan and bring to the boil. Pour over meat and marinate overnight. Depending on the age of the meat, stew or roast for 2 hours at 180°C (350°F) — if the meat is tough after roasting, then stew for an hour or until tender.

To make sauce, melt butter, add flour and stir until mixture browns. Add stock slowly, stirring vigorously until sauce thickens. Add jam. Serve sauce hot in sauce boat with roasted or stewed meat.

Note: This dish is traditionally served on its own, but can be eaten with the fresh vegetables of your choice.
Serves 6

RABBIT IN SOUR CREAM

KROLIK

1 rabbit, skinned and cleaned
1 cup vinegar
1 litre water
2 carrots, scraped
1 parsnip, scraped
2 onions, peeled
1 turnip, peeled
50 g butter
2 cups sour cream

Divide prepared rabbit into three pieces and place in a bowl (non-metal). Add vinegar and water to bowl, cover and set aside to marinate for 3–4 hours, then drain.

Place meat and vegetables in a casserole dish. Melt butter and pour over meat and vegetables. Bake at 180°C (350°F) for 1–1½ hours or until vegetables are cooked. Baste regularly with pan juices. Remove vegetables and arrange on a serving plate.

Make sauce by mixing sour cream with pan juices. Pour over meat, cover and roast for 30 minutes or until meat is tender. Serve meat with vegetables but on a separate plate.
Serves 4

ROAST DUCK AND KASHA

UTKA ZHARENAYA

1 medium-sized duck, cleaned
200 g duck giblets
20 g butter
1 cup cooked buckwheat kasha (see recipe)
1 cup water

Prepare duck by washing well inside and out under running water. Pan–fry duck giblets in butter until tender. Mix giblets and pan juices with kasha and use mixture to stuff the duck.

Place duck in a well-greased roasting pan. Add about a cup of water to pan and bake uncovered at 180°C (350°F) for 1½–2 hours. Baste several times during cooking with pan juices.
Serves 4

MINCED CHICKEN PATTIES

KOTLETY POZHARSKIE

5 slices stale white bread
½ cup milk
1 kg minced chicken meat
80–90 g butter
1 beaten egg
breadcrumbs
butter for frying

Soak bread in milk for about 30 minutes then squeeze dry. Mix chicken meat with bread, add butter and blend thoroughly.

With wet, clean hands, divide mixture into 6 equal parts and shape into patties. Dip each patty in egg, then roll in breadcrumbs.

Pan–fry in hot butter for about 5 minutes on each side. Pierce patties with a fork to check chicken colour. If liquid runs clear the chicken is cooked. Serve with Mustard Sauce (see recipe).
Serves 4–6

RABBIT MEAT BALLS

KOTLETY IZ KROLIKA

1 rabbit, skinned and cleaned
2 slices stale white bread soaked in milk
2 onions, peeled and chopped
3 eggs
1 cup breadcrumbs
4 tablespoons sunflower oil

Bone rabbit and press meat through a mincer twice. In a large mixing bowl, combine meat, bread, onion and 2 eggs until ingredients are thoroughly mixed and bound. Whisk remaining egg in a small deep plate. Place breadcrumbs in another similar plate.

Roll meat mixture between the palms into small balls about golf ball size. Roll each in egg, then breadcrumbs and lay out on a cool surface. Heat oil in frypan and cook about 10 meat balls at a time, turning constantly until golden brown, then place in a casserole dish. Bake in a slow oven 100°C (250°F) for 10 minutes.
Serves 8

Minced Chicken Patties

FISH AND SEAFOOD

There are many different styles of seafood dishes available — eaten as zakuski (appetisers) or as main meals.

Sturgeon is most well-known for producing the world's best caviar. The flesh of the sturgeon also makes excellent eating. It has a strong, rich flavour, similar to veal. If sturgeon is unavailable, substitute with a similar tasting fish, such as ling.

Cod and herring are found everywhere in the USSR and are considered to be an inexpensive meal.

The famous Chatka crab comes from the Kamchatka Peninsula and is a close relative to its neighbour, the giant Alaskan crab.

If you find salted herrings too salty, the simplest method of reducing the salty flavour is to soak them in a large bowl of water for at least two hours, changing the water once or twice.

SALMON WITH CHINESE VERMICELLI

SYEMGA S VIZIGOI

210 g can salmon
2 onions, peeled and chopped
40 g butter
100 g Chinese vermicelli or noodles
1 sprig fresh dill, finely chopped

Drain salmon. Fry onions in butter until soft but not brown. Add salmon. Stir–fry for 2 minutes.

Add vermicelli to a pan of boiling water and boil for 2 minutes. Drain in a colander.

Add to salmon mixture. Mix well and sprinkle with dill.
Serves 2

FISH SHASHLIK

4 tablespoons lemon juice
4 tablespoons sour cream
1 kg large firm-fleshed fish (cut in 5–6 cm chunks)

Combine lemon juice and cream. Dip each piece of fish in the sauce, then thread on skewers.

Cook under a griller for 7–8 minutes, turning constantly. When ready the fish will be brown. Score fish with a hot skewer.

Serve with pomegranate juice as for Shaslik with Pomegranate Juice. Serves 4–6

STURGEON IN SAUCE

OSETRINA S TOMATAMI I GRIBAMI

2 onions, peeled and chopped
1 carrot, scraped and grated
1 parsnip, scraped and grated
1 turnip, peeled and grated
425 g can peeled tomatoes
1 litre water
4 sturgeon fillets (see Note)
100 g mushrooms, chopped
3 tablespoons cream
1 tablespoon capers, drained
¾ cup green olives, stoned

Place first five ingredients into a large casserole dish, and cover with water. Bring to the boil, stirring vigorously then reduce heat and simmer for about 30 minutes until vegetables are cooked. Pass contents through a fine sieve and collect liquid. Press all vegetables to extract thin juices and discard pulp.

Put stock back in casserole dish, add fish fillets and bring to the boil. Reduce heat and simmer for 7–8 minutes. Remove fish and keep warm.

Boil stock again until it has reduced to about 500 mL. Empty mushrooms into the stock. Remove from heat and beat in cream slowly.

To serve, rinse olives to remove excess salt. Mix capers and olives into the sauce. Pour over fish and serve immediately.
Note: You can substitute with another full-flavoured fish, such as ling.

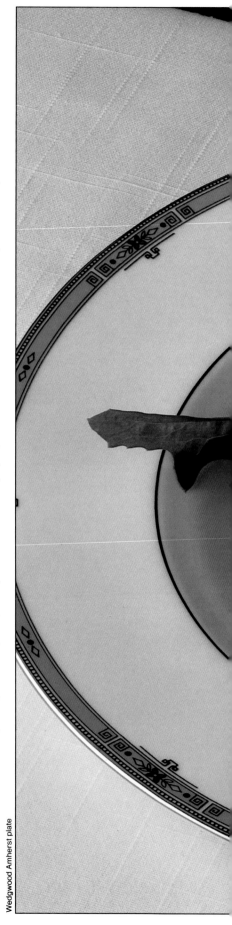

Fish Shashlik

Wedgwood Amherst plate

BAKED STURGEON
ZHARENNAYA OSETRINA

500–600 g sturgeon, scaled and
  cleaned (see Note)
20 g butter
½ cup water
juice ½ lemon

Place fish in a well-buttered
ovenproof dish and add about ½ cup
water. Cover and roast at 180°C
(350°F) for about 30 minutes. Baste
with pan juices and lemon juice. This
dish can be served with pan juices,
potato and lemon wedges.
Note: You may substitute with
another full-flavoured fish, such as
ling.
Serves 4

Marinated Fish with Carrots

Variations:

BAKED STURGEON WITH TOMATOES AND MUSHROOMS

100 g peeled tomatoes
200 g sliced mushrooms

Place in the dish with sturgeon and
roast as above. To serve, surround
fish with tomato and mushrooms and
pour pan juices over the fish.

BAKED STURGEON WITH POTATOES AND ONIONS

3 potatoes, peeled and finely sliced
1 large onion, peeled and sliced
40 g butter, melted
½ cup dry breadcrumbs

Place fish in dish as above. Arrange
slices of potato and onion alternately
to cover the upper surface of the fish.
Pour half the melted butter over the
vegetables and sprinkle with breadcrumbs. Pour over remaining butter
and bake as above.

MARINATED FISH WITH CARROTS
MARINOVANNAYA RYBA

1 kg mullet, cod or other similar fish
3 tablespoons flour
60 g butter
500 g carrots, scraped and julienned
3 large onions, peeled and cut into
  rings
1 kg tomatoes, peeled and finely
  chopped

Cut fish into pieces about 5 cm
square and dip each piece in flour.
Heat 30 g butter in a frypan and add
the fish pieces, skin side down. Cook
for 3 minutes, then turn and cook for
another 2 minutes.

Meanwhile bring carrots to the boil
in a small amount of water and simmer for 15 minutes. Remove carrots
and reserve cooking liquid.

Fry onions in remaining butter
until cooked but not brown. Sprinkle

1 tablespoon plain flour over onions. Add tomatoes and juice and stir constantly. Add 1 cup of carrot liquid to the tomato mixture.

Place carrots on the bottom of a casserole dish. Place the fish pieces on top and pour over the tomato–onion mixture. Cover the pan and simmer for 10 minutes. Serve hot or cold.
Serves 6

FRIED HERRINGS
ZHARENNAYA SELYODKA

2 salted herrings
2 tablespoons flour
40 g butter

Dip each herring into flour. Melt butter in pan and fry for a minute or two. Turn. Cover with sauce (see following recipes) and serve.
Serves 2

MUSTARD SAUCE

1 onion, finely chopped
20 g butter
1 tablespoon flour
1 tablespoon prepared mustard
3 tablespoons sour cream
1 sprig fresh dill, finely chopped

Fry onion in butter until soft but not brown. Add flour, stirring continuously. Then stir in all other ingredients and simmer until sauce thickens a little. Pour over herrings.
Serves 2

Fried Herrings with Tomato Sauce

TOMATO SAUCE

1 onion, finely chopped
20 g butter
2 tomatoes, skinned and finely chopped
2 tablespoons flour
1 sprig fresh dill, finely chopped

Fry onion in butter until soft but not brown. Add tomatoes and simmer for 2 minutes to reduce volume. Add flour, stirring constantly until thickened. Pour over herrings.
Serves 2

HERRING AND POTATO SALAD

SELYODKA S KARTOFELNYM SALATOM

4 large potatoes, peeled and quartered
1 cup fresh or frozen peas
½ cup fresh or frozen corn
2 salted herrings (soaked in water for half an hour)
1 cup sour cream

Place potatoes in a pan and cover with water. Bring to the boil and cook for 20 minutes or until soft. Remove potatoes with a slotted spoon.

Add peas and corn to the same cooking fluid. Bring to the boil, then turn heat off and drain.

Clean and bone herrings and cut into strips across the body about 1 cm wide.

Combine vegetables and herrings with sour cream and mix well. Allow to stand for approximately 30 minutes before serving.
Serves 4

BOILED HERRINGS WITH POTATOES

SELYODKA S KORTOSHKOI

2 salted herrings
4 large potatoes, peeled and quartered
1 sprig fresh dill, finely chopped

DRESSING (optional)
2 sprigs fresh dill, finely chopped and 40 g butter or
2 tablespoons grated horseradish and 2 tablespoons vinegar

Cover soaked herrings well with water and bring to the boil. Turn heat off.

Boil potatoes in water for 20 minutes.

Remove fish from pan and place on serving dish. Arrange potatoes around fish and sprinkle with dill.

To make dressing, combine dill and butter or horseradish and vinegar and serve separately.
Serves 2

HERRING STEWED IN MILK

SELYODKA TUSHENNAYA V MOLOKE

2 salted herrings, cleaned and soaked
1 cup milk
1 onion, peeled and chopped
1 bay leaf
4 sprigs fresh dill, finely chopped

Place soaked salted herrings in an elongated casserole dish or other suitable heatproof dish with milk, onion and bay leaf and bring to the boil. Simmer for 40–45 minutes, then remove fish and set aside.

Pass liquid through a fine sieve, add dill and mix well. Pour milk over the fish and serve.
Serves 2

EGGS AND CHEESE

Russian cooking uses a large number of eggs. They are used as binders in meat dishes, egg and breadcrumbs are used in many fried dishes and they are used liberally in baked goods and puddings. In the USSR, eggs can be bought by the carton of 100 rather than by the dozen.

A great variety of cheeses is available but yellow cheeses are rarely added to food. Their flavours and textures are enjoyed in the natural state. Cottage cheese, however, is used as a filling in pastry dishes, mixed with cereals and eaten by itself, either in its natural state or cooked. Most often it is combined with egg.

OMELETTE

OMLET

3 eggs
1 tablespoon milk
1 tablespoon flour
20 g butter

Beat eggs and milk. Mix in flour to form a batter. Heat butter in a cast iron frypan until pan is very hot.

Pour in mixture. As it starts to thicken, loosen edges with a knife and tilt frypan so that any liquid mixture may cook.

With a long–bladed spatula, loosen bottom of omelette and flip over.

FILLINGS

(1)
1 tablespoon finely chopped shallots
2 sprigs fresh dill, finely chopped

When omelette is cooked, place filling on one half and fold over to serve.

(2)
100 g stewed apple

Drain stewed apple and proceed as in (1).

(3)
½ cup cooked spinach or sorrel

Drain. Proceed as in (1).

(4)
1 boiled potato, sliced
1 sprig fresh dill, finely chopped

Mix potato with dill and proceed as in (1).

(5)
100 g fresh mushrooms
20 g butter

Fry mushrooms in butter. Add mushrooms to omelette and fold as in (1).
Serves 1

Variation:

CHEESE OMELETTE

50 g stale white bread
3 tablespoons milk
3 eggs
50 g cheese, grated
20 g butter

Soak bread in milk. Add eggs and cheese and beat until smooth.

Heat butter in cast iron frypan. Pour mixture into pan. Cook as for *Omelette* above. Alternatively, it can be placed in a slow oven 150°C (300°F) to set.

To make a fluffy omelette, separate egg whites and beat vigorously till stiff. Fold into mixture and combine as above.

COTTAGE CHEESE PATTIES

SYRNIKI

1 kg cottage cheese
5 egg yolks
300 g flour
2 tablespoons sugar
40 g butter
200 mL sour cream

Drain cottage cheese well, preferably overnight.

In a mixing bowl mix cottage cheese, egg yolks, flour and sugar. Shape into patties by rolling and shaping with the palms of the hands.

Fry patties in butter for about 2 minutes or until brown. Turn and fry the other side. The ideal cottage cheese patty has a fried crust and is soft in the middle.

Serve hot with sour cream poured over.
Serves 4

STUFFED EGGS

FARSHIROVANNYE YAITSA

5 eggs, hard-boiled
50 g stale white bread
½ cup milk
1 small onion, peeled and finely chopped
50 g sausage (luncheon sausage type), finely chopped
40 g butter
500 g potatoes, boiled
2 tablespoons milk
25 g cheese, grated

Cut eggs in half, lengthways. Remove yolks and carefully remove some of the white with a teaspoon to make a hollow.

Rub yolks with the back of a spoon till smooth. Finely chop the removed egg white and add to yolks.

Soak bread in ½ cup milk. Fry onion and sausage in half the butter. Squeeze bread dry. Mix with onion and sausage. Add to egg mixture.

Mash potatoes with 2 tablespoons milk. Add grated cheese.

Stuff eggs with bread-sausage mixture. With a wet knife cover the whole cut surface with mashed potato mixture so that the potato forms a shape of the half egg.

Brush with remaining butter and place under the griller until the potato is golden.
Serves 3

Cottage Cheese Patties

RUSSIAN YEAST COOKERY AND CEREALS

BREADS, PIES AND PASTRIES

Russian cooks have perfected yeast cookery, and Russians eat pies and pastries on all occasions. Modern Russian cuisine, as of old, is distinguished by its great variety of breads, pancakes, pies, porridge and gruels.

Piroshki are small, closed pies and patties or turnovers. There are many different kinds, and they can be either baked or deep–fried. Pirogi are large pies or tarts which can be closed, covered with a lattice pattern, or open.

The range of different breads available in Russia reflects the diversity characteristic of all Russian things. There are three major varieties: black breads, sweetened white breads and unsweetened white breads. Perhaps the most famous are the dark rye or black breads. Breads are distinguished not only by their flavour but also by shape, patterns and size, often determined by the occasion.

The secret of success with yeast cookery is the consistency of the pastry. Different–sized eggs produce batters of varying consistency and extra flour or milk may be needed. Experienced pastry cooks rarely need to measure ingredients accurately since they judge by the consistency of the batter or dough. Room temperature also has a critical bearing as it affects the way yeast rises. Doughs will rise faster in summer. A cool surface is needed for rolling out dough, for example, marble, but all ingredients should be at room temperature. The type of yeast used in the following recipes is compressed yeast.

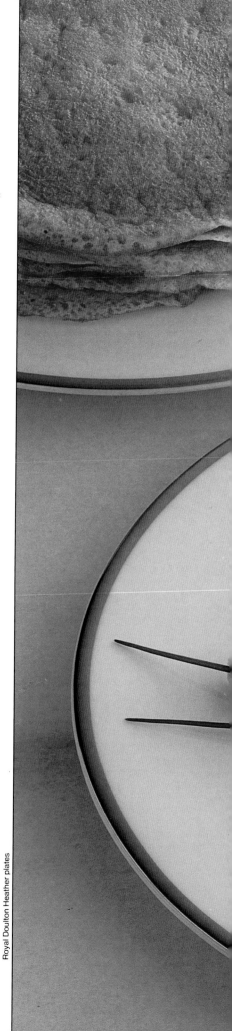

Royal Doulton Heather plates

Pancakes

Wedgwood Palatia plate

MEAT PIES
PIROSHKI

FILLINGS

(1)
800 g minced beef
40 g butter
2 onions, peeled and chopped
3 eggs, hard-boiled and chopped

Fry beef in butter until cooked but still tender. Add onion. Place in a mixing bowl. Add hard-boiled eggs and mix well.

(2)
2 cups water
1 cup toasted buckwheat
2 onions, peeled and chopped
40–60 g butter
3 eggs, hard-boiled and chopped

Add water to buckwheat in a pan. Bring to the boil and simmer for 15 minutes until fluffy and most of the water has been absorbed. Set aside.

Fry onions in butter until soft but not brown. Mix buckwheat, eggs and onions.

(3)
100 g Chinese vermicelli
3 hard-boiled eggs, choped
300 g smoked salmon or smoked
    cod, chopped

Boil noodles in water for about 3 minutes until transparent. Drain. Combine eggs, fish and noodles and mix well.

(4)
½ white cabbage, shredded
1 carrot, scraped and grated
3 eggs, hard-boiled
40 g butter
1 onion, peeled and chopped

Place a little water in frypan, add cabbage and stir on high heat until cabbage has wilted and the volume slightly decreased. Stir vigorously until no water remains. Add grated carrot and stir well, then cool.

Chop eggs finely, add butter, onion and cabbage mixture and mix well.

(5)
1 kg mushrooms, sliced
40 g butter
1 onion, peeled and chopped
¼ cup sour cream

Cook mushrooms in half the butter until tender. Fry onion in remaining butter and add sour cream. Add to mushrooms and simmer for 10–15 minutes.

Meat Pies 63

(6)
1 kg potatoes, peeled
40 g butter

Boil potatoes in water until soft. Mash with butter. Beat till very smooth.

(7)
500 g cottage cheese
2 eggs, beaten
20 g butter

Beat all ingredients together until creamy.

(8)
½ white cabbage, shredded
150 g almonds
100 g red capsicum, chopped finely
20 g marzipan

Place cabbage in a saucepan and add enough water to half cover it. Add almonds and capsicum. Bring to the boil and boil vigorously until well-cooked. Cool. Add marzipan and mix well.

(9)
½ white cabbage, shredded
1 cup cooked rice
½ cup sultanas

Cook cabbage as in (4). Mix with rice and sultanas.

(10)
300 g pitted cherries or raspberries
300 g strawberries
1 cup sugar, or to taste

Heat fruit and sugar in saucepan until thick. Be careful not to burn it.

(11)
500 g cottage cheese
1 cup stewed apple
sugar to taste

Press any excess moisture from cottage cheese. Drain apple. Mix cottage cheese, apple and sugar.

(12)
400 g almonds, finely chopped
300 g jam
100 g marzipan

Mix ingredients until smooth.

(13)
400 g fresh or frozen green beans, cooked
2 onions, peeled and sliced
2 tablespoons oil
4 sprigs fresh dill, finely chopped
black pepper

Fry beans and onions in oil, stirring constantly. Turn heat off. Add dill and pepper and mix well.

TO MAKE PIROSHKI

Roll the yeast pastry (see recipe) about 1 cm thick on a floured board. Cut out circles with a coffee mug. Gather scraps of pastry, roll into a ball and roll again. Set them aside to rise a little.

Place a large tablespoon of filling in each circle. Flatten filling with the back of the spoon. Fold pastry over the filling. Pinch the edges to seal. Place seam side down on a floured board, cover and set aside to rise for 10–15 minutes.

Heat 500 g lard or coconut fat or three-quarters fill a large saucepan with sunflower oil for deep frying.

Place 1 pie into the fat. If at right temperature, the fat should bubble and the pastry will brown in 1 minute or less. Turn. If the seal comes undone then the pastry contains too much fat.

When temperature is correct, place up to 6 piroshki in fat. It is difficult to control more than that number. When each is cooked, place on brown paper, kitchen towelling or similar fat–draining material. Allow to cool. Piroshki are served either as zakuski or as a main course.

YEAST PASTRY

30 g yeast
2½ cups warm milk
1 kg flour, sifted
100 g butter, melted
4 lightly beaten eggs
4 tablespoons sugar
1 teaspoon salt

In a large mixing bowl, mix yeast and warm milk, add half the flour and mix with a wooden spoon. Cover and set aside for 1 hour until batter has risen. It should about double in size.

Add butter, eggs, sugar and salt and mix with a wooden spoon. Fold in remaining flour and knead well until the dough forms a ball and leaves the sides of the bowl. Cover and set aside for 2 hours — again it should double in size.

Knead dough well for 3–4 minutes. Cover and set aside for 1 hour.

Makes about 35–40 piroshki

Yeast Pastry

1 Add half flour to yeast mixture with wooden spoon and allow to rise

2 Add butter, eggs, sugar and salt and fold in remaining flour

3 Knead well until dough forms a ball

PIES
PIROGI

Pirogi are large pies, baked as large flat sheets. Many different kinds of fillings can be used, such as dried apricots, apples, cottage cheese and carrots.

TO MAKE ONE LARGE PIE:
Make yeast pastry (see recipe) as for piroshki, but divide pastry into 2 halves. Roll each into a rectangle

large enough to cover bottom and sides of baking pan. The pastry should be about 1 cm thick. Spread with filling. Cover with other piece of pastry. Pinch edges to form a seal and brush with beaten egg. Pierce pastry with a fork in several places so the steam can escape. Carefully slide pirogi on to flat baking tray and bake for 45–55 minutes (depending on filling) at 180°C (350°F).

PIE PASTRY WITHOUT YEAST

2 eggs
300 g butter
2 tablespoons sugar
salt
2 cups self–raising flour
1 cup milk

Beat eggs in a mixing bowl. Add butter and sugar. Sift salt with flour. Add milk and flour alternately to make a dough which is soft. Too much flour will produce a stiff dough. Roll out on a floured board and proceed as above.

FILLINGS

(1)
8 pears
1 cup water
sugar to taste
2 cloves

Skin and core pears. Cut each into 4 pieces. Place in a saucepan together with other ingredients. Bring to the boil, stirring. Then simmer for about 10 minutes until soft and no water remains. Drain.

(2)
500 g grapes
¼ teaspoon nutmeg
1 cup water

Seed and peel grapes. Place in a saucepan with other ingredients, and cook as above.

All fillings cited for piroshki are suitable. Almost any combination of meat, fish, egg or cottage cheese with rice, buckwheat, cabbage, beans or onions can be used. A pie is an excellent dish for using up leftovers.

PANCAKES (1)
BLINY

Traditionally buckwheat flour is used, but plain flour can be substituted.

40 g yeast
2 cups warm water
1 kg flour, sifted
salt
2 tablespoons sugar
2 lightly beaten eggs
60 g butter, melted
4–5 cups warm milk

Dissolve yeast in water and add 500 g flour. Mix until smooth, cover with a cloth and set aside for about 1 hour or until the batter becomes bubbly.

Add salt, sugar, eggs and butter and mix thoroughly. Gradually add the remaining flour and beat until smooth. Add milk gradually, the batter should be quite runny. Cover with a cloth and set aside. When batter rises, beat it again and set aside to rise further. The batter should be set aside for at least 30 minutes before cooking.

Heat a long-handled frypan, ensuring that the bottom is perfectly smooth and clean. Rub over base of pan with 20 g butter enclosed in a small clean cloth.

Use a soup ladle to pour batter into pan. One ladle will be adequate. Cook for 1 minute and flip over. Cook 1 minute more. Slide out of pan onto a flat plate. Stack one on top of another to keep warm. Rub greased cloth over pan bottom before adding batter each time.

Makes approximately 30

Pancakes served with Sour Cream and Caviar

Royal Doulton Heather plate

PANCAKES (2)
BLINY

3 eggs
2½ cups milk
salt
250 g flour, sifted
40 g butter, melted

Beat egg yolks, add ½ cup milk and salt. Gradually mix in the flour with a wooden spoon. Add butter. Beat until smooth. Gradually add remaining milk and beaten egg whites. Cook in long-handled frypan as for (1). Serve with the filling of your choice.

FILLINGS

(1) Meat filling as for piroshki

Place meat in centre and fold pancake around meat like an envelope.

Stack in a greased casserole dish and heat gently at 100°C (200°F) for 20 minutes.

(2) Cottage cheese

Place cottage cheese in centre of pancake and follow directions as for Filling (1).

(3) Apple

Reconstitute dried apple rings. Cook according to directions. Drain. Proceed as for Filling (1).

(4) AUSTRALIAN VARIATIONS

Vegemite

Spread over whole surface and simply roll up tightly.

Apple and cinnamon

Prepare dried apple as for Filling (1). Add 1 teaspoon cinnamon.

Orange Butter and Grand Marnier

Melt 40 g butter. Add 1 tablespoon freshly squeezed orange juice and residual pulp. Mix well. Spread pancake onto a dinner plate. Flame alcohol and add to butter, mixing just before serving. Fold pancake over in half and pour orange mixture over pancake.

Smoked Salmon

Place smoked salmon in centre of pancake and follow directions as for Fillings (1).

Sour Cream and Caviar

Place sour cream and caviar in centre of pancake and follow directions as for Fillings (1).

YEAST BUNS
BULOCHKI

40 g yeast
1½ cups milk, warmed
1 kg flour, sifted
½ teaspoon salt
5 egg yolks
1½ cups sugar
300 g butter, melted

Dissolve yeast in warm milk in a large mixing bowl. Mix in half the flour, cover with a cloth and set aside until doubled in size. Beat together salt, egg yolks and sugar and add to the dough. Add remaining flour and mix well. Knead.

Add melted butter and mix. Knead well until the dough forms a ball. Good kneading produces light, well risen buns. Cover and set aside. When dough has doubled in size turn out on a floured board.

Pull off about a tablespoon of dough to shape for each bun. Place dough on greased baking tray leaving at least 6 cm spaces between them for the buns to rise. Set baking tray aside for dough to rise — about 30 minutes.

Preheat oven to hot 220°C (425°F). Immediately on placing dough in oven, reduce heat to 180°C (350°F) and bake for 10 minutes. Buns will be golden and springy to touch when done.
Makes 15–20 buns

FLAT ARMENIAN BREAD
CHUREK

40 g yeast
2 cups warm water
1 kg flour, sifted
130 g butter, melted
1 tablespoon sugar
2 teaspoons salt
2 tablespoons sesame seeds

Dissolve yeast in a little of the water in a small bowl. Cover with a cloth and set aside for 5–10 minutes until mixture begins to bubble. Place flour in a large mixing bowl, making a well in the centre. Add yeast mixture, remaining water, butter, sugar and salt. Mix with a wooden spoon. Then knead for 10 minutes until dough is soft. Cover with a cloth and set aside for about 30 minutes until dough doubles in size.

Preheat oven to 200°C (400°F). Divide dough into 10 pieces. Roll out each piece of a floured board. Each circle should be quite thin. Place 2 circles on a baking tray at a time. Brush lightly with water and sprinkle sesame seeds on the top. Bake for 20–25 minutes until golden brown.

Cool thoroughly and keep dry. The bread will keep for a few days in the same way as ordinary bread or can be frozen under the same conditions as commercial bread.
Makes 10

Left to right: Flat Armenian Bread
Yeast Buns

KULICH
KULICH

Kulich is a very traditional type of sweet bread full of spices. It has a wonderful aroma and has good keeping quality. The shape is traditional and is eaten with Paskha (see recipe) which is a sweet cottage cheese dessert.

40–50 g yeast
1½ cups warm milk
1 kg flour, sifted
½ teaspoon salt
6 eggs
1½ cups sugar
300 g butter
200 g raisins
50 g candied peel, finely chopped
50 g almond meal
5–6 ground cardamom seeds
¼ teaspoon nutmeg
¼ teaspoon cinnamon
½ teaspoon powdered saffron
½ teaspoon vanilla essence or vanilla pod

In a large mixing bowl, dissolve yeast in warm milk, stir in half the flour and mix till smooth. Cover with a cloth to rise. When dough has doubled, add salt, egg yolks, leaving a small amount to brush the top. Add sugar and butter. Mix well. Beat egg whites till stiff and fold into the mixture alternately with remaining flour. Continue mixing until the dough can be formed into a ball and does not stick to the sides of the bowl. Cover and set aside. When dough has again doubled add raisins, candied peel, almond meal, spices and vanilla. Mix very well. It is traditional to serve a kulich with a pink rose.

The dough should be baked in tins which are round and tall. The height should be greater than the diameter. Old tin cannisters are ideal, 15–20 cm diameter and 25–30 cm tall.

Butter pieces of greaseproof paper on both sides and line bottom and sides of tin allowing paper to protrude up to 4–5 cm above the tin.

Fill the tin about one-third full. Cover and set aside. When the dough has risen to about three-quarters full (which should take about 30 minutes), brush top with beaten egg. Preheat the oven to 180°C (350°F) and bake for 50–60 minutes. The top will rise over the tin like a mushroom. If it begins to burn, cover top with the same paper used for lining the tin.

When ready, the kulich should be a golden colour. Test with a straw. If it comes out clean, the kulich is cooked. Remove from oven and let stand for 5 minutes to cool. Place tin on its side and pull the paper lining. Paper and kulich should emerge easily. Place it upright on a cake rack to cool.

This recipe should make 2 large kulich. Smaller ones are traditionally given as gifts. Use tin from canned fruit or coffee. Remove the paper labels and check that container is safe to heat. Cook smaller kulich 40–50 minutes or until golden brown.

TRADITIONAL KULICH ICING
Mazurka

1 piece clean muslin or cotton 20–25 cm square
2 cups icing sugar
2 egg whites, beaten until very stiff
1 teaspoon strained lemon juice

Arrange muslin square on a cold flat surface. Mix icing sugar with egg whites and lemon juice.

With a wet knife working quickly, spread the mixture over the material thickly and evenly. Allow to settle for about 5 minutes then drape over the kulich. Often a cut-out border to give a lace effect is made. The top should set very hard. Take care not to crack the icing when removing muslin for serving. It should slide off mushroom top easily.

To serve, cut mushroom cap off kulich. Then cut crossways about 2 cm thick and then into quarters. The cap can then be replaced without obvious disturbance.

FAMILY KULICH
KULICH DOMASHNYI

50 g yeast
1 cup milk
950 g flour
25 egg yolks
250 g sugar
1 teaspoon salt
200 g butter
25 g candied citrus peel, finely chopped
10 g lemon rind, grated
20 mL rum or cognac
½ teaspoon vanilla

In a large mixing bowl, dissolve yeast in ½ cup warm milk, stir in 100 g flour and mix till smooth. Cover with a cloth and leave to rise.

Meanwhile heat ½ cup milk to boiling point until bubbles just start appearing and mix in 100 g flour with wooden spoon. Cool to room temperature. Add to yeast mixture in bowl, mix well, cover, and leave to rise for 2 hours.

In a separate mixing bowl, beat yolks with sugar and salt until sugar has dissolved. Divide mixture in half. Add one half to the risen dough together with 250 g flour. Mix well. Allow to stand for 1 hour.

Melt butter and add candied peel, lemon rind, rum and vanilla and 500 g flour. When dough has risen, add this to mixture together with remaining half of yolk and sugar mixture. Knead dough well until it no longer sticks to the hands. Allow to rise for 1–1½ hours.

The dough should be baked in tins which are round and tall. The height should be greater than the diameter. Tin canisters 15–20 cm diameter and 25–30 cm tall are ideal. Use baking paper, or butter pieces of grease-proof paper on both sides and line bottom and sides of tins, allowing paper to protrude up to 4–5 cm above the rim. Half fill tins with dough.

Leave dough to rise until tin is about ¾ full. Bake in a moderate oven 180°C (350°F) until golden brown. The smaller the tins the quicker the Kulich will cook. One small loaf tin of dough takes about 30 minutes, while a large tin takes 1½–2 hours.

Makes 1 large kulich or 4 small loaf tins

Kulich

MEAT DUMPLINGS (1)
PELMENI

PASTRY
330 g flour, sifted
1 teaspoon salt
4 egg yolks
2 cups warm milk

Sift flour and salt into a large mixing bowl and make a well in the centre. Whisk egg yolks and milk and pour into well. Slowly, with a wooden spoon fold in flour until the dough forms a ball. Knead well. Cover with a cloth and set aside for about 30 minutes.

Transfer dough to floured board and knead again. Dough should be very smooth. Add extra flour if necessary. Roll out until thin. Cut into small rounds about 5–6 cm in diameter.

Place about 1 small teaspoon prepared filling (see recipe) on dough round and fold over. Pinch edges to seal, pull out ends to form horns and curl under base of dumpling.

Fold under 2 end tails closest to folded edge so that they touch. Place on floured board with tails underneath until ready to cook.

Half fill a large saucepan with stock (see below) and bring to the boil. Drop in about 10 pelmeni at a time. Simmer for 5–10 minutes or until they rise to the surface. Use a large perforated spoon to remove when cooked. Drain.

FILLING

500 g beef or pork, minced
1 onion, peeled and finely chopped
3 tablespoons cold water
  (approximately)

Mix thoroughly. Do not cook. Place on dough and proceed as described.

STOCK

(1)
Meat stock (see recipe)
(2)
Bone stock (see recipe)
(3)
1 tablespoon vegemite dissolved in required amount of water
(4)
1 tablespoon soy sauce in required amount of water

Pelmeni are served with stock in a large soup plate or separately without stock.

GARNISH

1 tablespoon grated cheese sprinkled over each individual serve
1 tablespoon vinegar may be added to individual serve of stock

Pelmeni freeze well. In Russia they were stored in the snow. Place in a plastic bag and freeze. When required *do not thaw*. Drop frozen pelmeni into boiling stock.
Makes about 40–50 or 4 large portions.

Variations:

DUMPLINGS WITH COTTAGE CHEESE
VARENIKI

FILLING
500 g cottage cheese
1 egg
1 tablespoon sugar
200 mL sour cream

Prepare pastry as for (1).

Mix together cottage cheese, egg and sugar. Place on pastry round and seal in the usual manner. Boil in water instead of stock.

Serve with sour cream. Extra sugar may be added.

DEEP–FRIED LAMB DUMPLINGS

500 g lamb, minced
1 onion, peeled and finely chopped
2 tablespoons cooked rice
1 egg, beaten
oil for deep–frying

Prepare pastry as for (1).

Mix together lamb, onion, rice and beaten egg. Make dumplings. Seal well and brush with beaten egg.

Heat oil and fry dumplings for 2–3 minutes. Turn. They should be golden brown. Do not cook more than 5 or 6 at once. Drain and serve with soup.

FRUIT–FILLED DUMPLINGS

600 g pitted cherries, strawberries, blueberries or pitted plums
200 g sugar, or as required

Wash fruit. Place in a saucepan with sugar and bring to the boil, stirring constantly. Take care that it does not burn.

Prepare pastry, add fruit filling and proceed as for (1). Serve with extra fruit filling.

Fruit-filled Dumplings

Flaky Pastry

1 Rub butter into flour

2 Place dobs of butter over top two-thirds of pastry and fold up bottom third

3 Roll out and repeat procedure

FLAKY PASTRY

230 g flour
¼ teaspoon salt
170 g butter
¼ cup cold water
½ teaspoon lemon juice

Sift flour and salt into a mixing bowl.

Divide butter into 4. Rub one-quarter of the butter into the flour. Add water and lemon juice and mix to a soft dough.

Roll out the pastry on a floured board into an oblong, about 3 times as long as wide.

Cut another quarter of the butter into pieces and place over the top two-thirds of the pastry. Fold the bottom third up and the top third down. Then roll the pastry so that the edges become sealed and the pastry has elongated. Add another quarter of butter and refold. Repeat procedure until all butter is used.

Wrap dough in greaseproof paper and refrigerate for 1 hour.

Makes enough dough for one large baking tray

STREUDEL WITH PEARS AND APPLES

3 apples
3 pears
1 tablespoon sour cream
black pepper
1 sprig dill, finely chopped

Peel and core apples and pears and cut into quarters. Place them in a saucepan with a little water, bring to the boil and simmer for 10 minutes or until soft. Drain. Combine with remaining ingredients in a mixing bowl. Spread on pastry and proceed as for Russian Streudel (see recipe following).

Serve with extra sour cream. Garnish with pear and apple.

Streudel with Pears and Apples

Wedgwood Silver Ermine plate

RUSSIAN STREUDEL (1)
STRUDEL

flaky pastry (see recipe)

FILLING
200 g topside steak, minced
1 onion, peeled and minced
20 g butter
*150 g walnuts, cleaned and finely
    chopped*
1 egg
*fresh young spinach and dill, finely
    chopped*

Fry topside and onion in butter, cool. In a mixing bowl, combine walnuts, egg and greens with the meat mixture. Thoroughly blend all ingredients.

Roll out pastry on a floured board into a thin rectangle, 3–4 mm thick. Spread filling evenly over pastry stopping 1 cm from all edges.

Roll up tightly taking care not to break the pastry. Brush end seam with egg to seal. Place on a flat oven tray and bake at 220°C (425°F) for 20–25 minutes.

Variations:

STREUDEL WITH CORN

200 g fresh or canned sweet corn
1 egg

Cook corn according to directions. Drain and cool. Mix in egg. Spread on pastry and proceed as for (1).

STREUDEL WITH MUSHROOMS, SAUSAGE AND GARLIC

300 g mushrooms
40 g butter
200 g sliced sausage
1 clove garlic
flaky pastry (see recipe)

Wash and fry mushrooms in butter until cooked. Finely chop all ingredients and mix well. Set prepared flaky pastry aside for 30 minutes, then roll out 1–2 mm thick. If pastry breaks, add extra flour. Spread on pastry and bake as for (1).

STREUDEL WITH COTTAGE CHEESE

300 g cottage cheese
25 g sultanas
2 eggs
40 g butter
1 tablespoon sugar

Press and drain any excess moisture from cottage cheese. Place all ingredients in a mixing bowl. Beat until smooth. Spread on pastry and proceed as for (1).

STREUDEL WITH QUINCE

3 quinces
1 cup canned pitted cherries
flaky pastry (see recipe)
40 g butter

Peel and core quinces. Grate coarsely. Drain cherries, reserving the juice.

Set prepared flaky pastry aside for 30 minutes. Roll out pastry 1–2 mm thick. If pastry breaks, add extra flour.

Add butter to quinces and cherries and mix well. Spread on pastry and proceed as for (1).

When streudel is cooked, allow to cool. With a spoon pour cherry juice over pastry so that it is saturated.

STREUDEL WITH CANDIED PEEL

200 g candied peel
300 g candied apricots
200 g candied pears
2 rings candied pineapple
50 g icing sugar
flaky pastry (see recipe)

Chop fruit very finely and mix well. Set prepared flaky pastry aside for 30 minutes then roll out 1–2 mm thick. If pastry breaks, add extra flour. Spread on pastry and bake.

While still hot sprinkle streudel with icing sugar.

STREUDEL WITH RICE, PEARS, SULTANAS AND CARROTS

3 pears
150 g sultanas
2 carrots, scraped and grated
1 cup cooked rice
1 tablespoon icing sugar
½ teaspoon vanilla essence

Peel and core pears and cut into quarters. Bring to the boil in a little water and simmer for 10 minutes or until soft. Switch off heat, add sultanas and carrots, keep lid on for 3 minutes and then drain.

Place rice, icing sugar and vanilla in a bowl and mix. Add drained ingredients and mix well. Spread on pastry and proceed as for (1).

STREUDEL WITH HONEY AND POPPY SEEDS

40 g butter
300 g poppy seeds
flaky pastry (see recipe)
2–3 tablespoons honey
50 g nuts, finely chopped

Melt butter and add poppy seeds. Place in refrigerator for about 30 minutes to cool and harden slightly. Set prepared pastry aside for 30 minutes then roll out 1–2 mm thick. If pastry breaks, add extra flour. Spread over pastry and bake as for (1).

When streudel is cool, heat honey carefully until a pouring consistency. Take care not to burn. Pour over streudel to saturate. Sprinkle chopped nuts on top.

Note: Other fillings include meats, root vegetables or greens (such as cabbage or turnip tops), sauerkraut, and any preserved fruits or mushrooms.

CEREALS (KASHA)

Cereal is an important staple food in the Russian diet. More use is made of cereals there than in the West, and more varieties are available. They are eaten any time of the day, either with meat or egg dishes or as a complete meal.

Cereal dishes are called 'kasha' which translates into porridge. Buckwheat is very popular, but it is different from the product available here — toasted buckwheat is the most similar. Often buckwheat is sold untoasted so it is best to toast it on a flat baking dish in a slow oven taking care not to burn it. Cereals can hold a lot of heat, so they char suddenly and quickly burn. Buckwheat groats from the USA are most like the tasty Russian buckwheat.

Vegetable–cereal combinations are popular and have been shown to be nutritionally desirable. The correct combinations provide protein equivalent in quality to animal protein.

Timing for the cooking of these cereals is not critical. The times quoted here generally produce a chewy product. More time can be given if a softer texture is preferred.

BUCKWHEAT KASHA (1)

GRECHNEVAYA KASHA S MASLOM

3 cups water
2 cups buckwheat
40 g butter

Place water in a saucepan and bring to the boil. Add buckwheat and simmer for 15–20 minutes. The grain will become soft and increase in volume. Reduce heat to a very low simmer, cover and keep warm for 1–2 hours. Serve with butter.
Serves 4–6

Variations:

BUCKWHEAT KASHA WITH COTTAGE CHEESE

BITOCHKI C TVOROGOM

1 cup buckwheat
1½ cups water
200 g cottage cheese
2 eggs
2 tablespoons sugar
½ cup dry breadcrumbs
40 g butter
sour cream to taste

Cook buckwheat as for (1). Add cottage cheese, eggs and sugar and mix well. Shape into balls. Dip in breadcrumbs and fry in butter. Serve with sour cream.

BUCKWHEAT KASHA WITH MUSHROOMS

GRECHNEVAYA KASHA S GRIBAMI

2½ cups buckwheat
3 cups water
1 cup fresh mushrooms, sliced
40 g butter
sour cream to taste

Cook buckwheat as for (1). Fry mushrooms in butter and for 4 minutes. Add mushrooms to buckwheat, cover and bake for 20 minutes at 100°C (200°F). Serve with sour cream.

WHEAT PORRIDGE

PSHYONNAYA KASHA

4 tablespoons First-break wheat (see Note)
600 mL milk
sugar
salt

Mix wheat in cold milk and bring to the boil. Simmer for 15–20 minutes, stirring constantly. Add sugar and salt to taste.
Note: First-break wheat is the lightly crushed wheat seed.
Serves 2

RICE PORRIDGE

RISOVAYA KASHA

4 cups water
2 cups rice
40–60 g butter

Boil water in a pan, add rice and simmer until porridge thickens, stirring constantly. Cover. Turn off heat. Let stand for 50 minutes. Mix in butter before serving hot.
Serves 4–6

MAIZE PORRIDGE

KASHA IZ KUKURUZY

1 cup water
1 cup maize
2 cups milk
2 tablespoons melted butter
1 tablespoon sugar

Bring water to the boil in a saucepan, add maize and cook for 10–15 minutes. Add milk and cook mixture a further 15–20 minutes. To serve, pour butter over kasha and sprinkle with sugar.
Serves 4

GEORGIAN PILAU

PLOV PO-GRUZINSKI

2 cups rice
2 cups water
150 g honey
150 g raisins
125 g butter, melted

Cook rice in boiling water as for rice porridge. Measure honey and dilute with an equal volume of warm water. Add raisins and butter to the mixture. Pour over rice and heat in a 150°C (300°F) oven for 10 minutes.
Serves 4–6

RICE WITH PUMPKIN

ZAPEKANKA

1 cup rice
2 cups water
2 cups cooked pumpkin, mashed
2 eggs
60 g butter
½ teaspoon cinnamon
½ teaspoon nutmeg

Cook rice as for rice porridge. In a mixing bowl, mix rice, pumpkin, eggs, butter and spices.

Spoon the mixture into a greased casserole dish. Bake in a 180°C (350°F) oven for 15 minutes. Turn oven off and keep hot for another 15 minutes.
Serves 4–6

PUMPKIN AND FRUIT PILAU

PLOV S TYKVOI I FRUKTAMI

500 g pumpkin, cooked and mashed
200 g apples, peeled and sliced
100 g quince, peeled and diced
100 g raisins
1 tablespoon water
1½ cups cooked rice
½ cup melted butter

In a saucepan combine pumpkin, fruits and raisins with water. Bring to the boil, remove from heat and mix well.

Arrange rice on platter. Pour saucepan ingredients over rice and top with melted butter.
Serves 4–6

MACARONI (1)

MAKARONY

1 cup macaroni
2 eggs
1 tablespoon sugar
200 g cottage cheese
20 g butter

Cover macaroni with water and bring to the boil. Boil for 10 minutes, until *al dente*, then drain.

In a mixing bowl, mix eggs, sugar, cottage cheese and butter. Add macaroni.

Spoon mixture into a greased casserole dish. Bake in a 180°C (350°F) oven for 20–25 minutes.
Serves 3–4

Variation:

MACARONI WITH GIBLETS

1 cup macaroni
2 eggs
1 onion peeled
40 g butter
300 g giblets, chopped

Cook macaroni as for (1) and drain. Add eggs. Fry onion in butter but do not brown. Add giblets and fry, stirring vigorously. Add macaroni to frypan and stir well. Fry for 5 minutes. Cover and allow to stand for 10 minutes before serving.
Serves 3–4

SEMOLINA (1)

MANNAYA KASHA

1 cup semolina
1 tablespoon sugar
5 cups milk

Add semolina and sugar to cold milk. Stir well. Bring to the boil. Simmer for about 10 minutes stirring continuously until thick.
Serves 4–6

DESSERT SEMOLINA

GURYEVSKAYA KASHA

¾ cup semolina
3 tablespoons sugar
2 cups milk
40 g butter
2 tablespoons ground almonds
¼ teaspoon vanilla essence
2 eggs
1 tablespoon sugar extra

TO SERVE
50 g blanched almonds
fresh or canned fruit

Cook semolina and sugar in milk as for (1). When cooked add butter, ground almonds, vanilla, and eggs. Mix well.

Place into individual baking dishes, sprinkle with sugar (see *Note*) and bake at 180°C (350°F) for approximately 15 minutes or till golden brown. When baked score the top with a hot skewer.

To serve, roast blanched almonds and chop finely. Sprinkle over the top. Serve with fruit and almonds.
Note: Traditionally this dessert is very sweet and the extra sprinkled sugar is optional.
Serves 4–6

DESSERTS, SWEETS AND DRINKS

BISCUITS AND CAKES

The cakes and sweet pastries of Russia are an art form. Dessert recipes have also been influenced by French and other European cuisines, as well as those of Middle Eastern and Moslem countries.

The modern Russian woman, like women everywhere, has less time to spend in the kitchen. However, there will always be occasions when time can be found to bake something festive and special.

BISCUITS

KORZHIKI

2 cups flour
3 tablespoons sugar
½ teaspoon bicarbonate of soda
¼ teaspoon salt
1 egg
⅔ cup sour cream
40 g butter

Sift dry ingredients into a mixing bowl. Make a well in the middle, drop in the egg and mix. Add sour cream and butter and beat well. Roll out on a floured board and cut into biscuit shapes.

Place on a greased oven sheet. Brush with beaten egg and pierce with a fork in several places. Bake in a 220°C (425°F) oven for 10–15 minutes until brown.
Serves 6–8

Biscuits

ALMOND BISCUITS
KRENDEL C MINDALEM

40 g yeast
1 ½ cups milk
1 kg flour, sifted
12 egg yolks
1 ½ cups sugar
¼ teaspoon vanilla essence
300 g butter
½ teaspoon salt
200 g raisins
100 g toasted almonds, chopped
½ cup icing sugar

Mix yeast, milk and half the flour, cover and set aside for 10 minutes.

Beat egg yolks, sugar and vanilla until sugar is dissolved. Add butter.

When the yeast mixture is bubbling, add to egg mixture, beating well. Add remaining flour and salt.

Knead the dough until it leaves the sides of the bowl. Add raisins, knead and set aside, covered, in a warm place. Allow to stand until dough has just about doubled in size. This is a heavy dough and will not rise as much as lighter yeast doughs.

Knead and roll on a floured board and roll out like a sausage but tapering at both ends. Tie to form a knot or a bow.

Place on a greased flat baking sheet and set aside, covered in a warm place for about 10 minutes. Brush with egg yolk and sprinkle with chopped almonds. Bake in a 180°C (350°F) oven for 40–50 minutes until golden brown. Allow to cool.

Sift icing sugar twice. Sprinkle icing sugar quite heavily over krendel so that the top is white.

Serves 6–8

COOKIES
PRYANIKI

1 egg
1 cup sugar
6 cardamom seeds, ground
½ teaspoon lemon rind, grated
1 cup flour, sifted

Beat egg with sugar until sugar has dissolved. Add cardamom and lemon rind.

Fold in the flour and beat until smooth. On a flat, greased oven tray drop the batter from a teaspoon, allowing room to spread — about 3–4 cm. Bake in a 220°C (425°F) oven for 8 minutes.

Serves 4–6

POPPY SEED CAKES
KEKS S MAKOM

50 g yeast
100 mL warm water
100 g sugar
650 g flour, sifted
100 g butter
1 tablespoon sunflower oil
3 eggs
½ teaspoon salt
100 g poppy seeds

Add yeast to warm water and mix in 15 g sugar. Add flour and mix well. Set aside, covered for 1 hour.

Meanwhile, in another mixing bowl, beat butter, oil, eggs, remaining sugar and salt until sugar is dissolved and the batter is frothy. Add this to yeast mixture and mix well. Add poppy seeds, reserving a few for garnish, and again beat well.

Spoon mixture into greased, floured patty tins. Set aside, covered to rise for 10–15 minutes. Sprinkle with poppy seeds. Bake at 200°C (400°F) for 15 minutes or until golden brown.

Serves 6

MOLDAVIAN CAKES
KEKS MOLDAVSKII

210 mL milk
440 g flour, sifted
40 g yeast
4 eggs, separated
260 g sugar
¼ teaspoon vanilla
50 g butter
2 tablespoons sunflower oil
20 g sultanas
30 g candied peel

Mix yeast in 2 tablespoons of the warm milk and add 4 tablespoons flour. Mix well. Set aside in a warm place, covered for 2–3 hours.

Bring 120mL milk to the boil, cool and add to yeast mixture and mix well. In another saucepan, dissolve 160 g of sugar in remaining milk. Add 4 yolks, vanilla, pinch of salt, mix well. Heat and add to the mixture above.

Add remaining flour and knead into a stiff dough.

Heat butter and add to oil. Heat mixture so that it is lukewarm and well mixed. Slowly add to dough and knead. Add sultanas and candied peel and knead again till well mixed. Set aside, covered, in a warm place for 3 hours.

Roll out dough on a floured board. Hand roll pieces of dough (1–2 tablespoons each) into small balls. Place these balls into greased and floured patty tins and leave 1–1½ hours, covered, to rise.

Just before baking, brush tops of cakes with egg yolk and sprinkle with sugar.

Bake in a 180°C (350°F) oven for about 20 minutes or until done.

Serves 6–8

Honey Cake

HONEY CAKE
KOVRIZHKA

1 egg
½ cup sugar
150 g honey
cinnamon, to taste
cloves, to taste
½ teaspoon bicarbonate of soda
2 cups flour, sifted
50 g blanched almonds

Beat egg and sugar together. Add honey, spices and bicarbonate of soda. Gradually fold in flour. Pour into a greased, floured square cake tin.

Decorate the top of the cake with almonds and bake in a preheated 180°C (350°F) oven for 15–20 minutes.

When cool, the cake may be cut into 2 layers. Fill with jam.
Serves 10

HONEY BISCUITS
MEDOVYE PRYANIKI

4 eggs
2 cups sugar
500 g honey
½ teaspoon vanilla essence
1 kg flour
2 teaspoons bicarbonate of soda
¼ teaspoon cinnamon
¼ teaspoon nutmeg
icing sugar and cinnamon

Beat eggs and sugar until thick. Add honey and vanilla and mix well. Sift flour, soda, cinnamon and nutmeg and fold into mixture. Set aside, covered for 24 hours. Dough should be stiff. Roll out to a flat sheet. Either cut into shapes or roll up tightly and cut into widths 10–15 mm thick.

Bake on a greased baking tray in an oven at 190°C (375°F) for 15 minutes. Dust with icing sugar and cinnamon.
Serves 6–8

WALNUT CAKE
TORT S GRETSKIMI OREKHAMI

10 eggs
150 g sugar
2 cups walnuts, shelled and cleaned
4 tablespoons soft breadcrumbs
2 tablespoons self–raising flour, sifted
whipped cream

Beat egg yolks with sugar until thick. Separately whip egg whites until stiff. Fold into mixture. Add walnuts and mix well. Fold in breadcrumbs and flour and mix well.

Pour into a large, greased and floured tin and bake in a 180°C (350°F) oven for 30–35 minutes or until golden brown. Cover with whipped cream.
Serves 6–8

Honey Biscuits

Royal Doulton Heather plate   Sasaki cutlery

RUM BABA
ROMOVAYA BABA

50 g yeast
2 cups milk, warmed
1 kg flour
¾ teaspoon salt
7 eggs
1 ¼ cups sugar
½ teaspoon vanilla essence
300 g butter
200 g sultanas

SYRUP
½ cup sugar
1 ¾ cups water
4–6 tablespoons red wine, liqueur or 1 tablespoons rum essence

Mix yeast with 1 cup warm milk. Add 3 cups plain flour and mix with a wooden spoon to a stiff batter. Roll into a ball.

On one side make 5 or 6 shallow cuts. Place the batter in a saucepan containing 2–2½ litres warm water. Cover with a lid and set aside in a warm place.

In 45 minutes–1 hour, when dough has doubled in size, remove from water. Place dough in a mixing bowl, add 1 cup warm milk, salt, egg yolks, sugar and vanilla essence. Beat egg whites till stiff and add to mixture, blending well. Add remaining flour and knead dough well.

Add butter and knead well again. The dough should be pliable and not too stiff. Cover and set aside until doubled in size.

Add sultanas and mix well. Line a loaf tin of the same type that is used in the recipe for Kulich with grease-proof paper, with the paper projecting up over the top. Fill the tin to one-third with batter, set aside and cover until batter three-quarter fills the tin. Preheat the oven to 180°C (350°F).

Very carefully, place baba into oven. Turn baba at intervals so that it get adequate heat. If the baba is knocked it can collapse. If it is not turned it may become hollow in the middle. Bake for 45 minutes to 1 hour.

When baked, carefully remove the baba, remove from tin and place on its side when cool.

Combine all ingredients to make syrup. Pour syrup very evenly over the baba until all syrup is used.

Place paper doiley over the top of the baba and put on the table as a centrepiece before eating the dessert. It should not stay in the open air for more than one hour as it will lose its wonderful aroma.
Serves 8–10

EASY METHOD:
Instead of using a kulich cake tin, divide mixture into patty tins. Set aside and cover until dough doubles in size.

Place in oven, cook for 30 minutes or until done. Saturate individual babas with syrup.

BABAS
BABA

WITH CHOCOLATE

10 egg yolks
130 g butter
250 g caster sugar
¼ teaspoon vanilla essence
100 g cooking chocolate, grated
½ cup milk
150 g almonds, toasted and finely chopped

Beat egg yolks into butter, one yolk at a time. Add sugar and vanilla. In one direction only, mix well. Dissolve grated chocolate in milk. Add with almonds to mixture, still only beating in the one direction.

Place in a large greased, floured loaf tin and cook in a 180°C (350°F) oven for 45 minutes.

It is served either iced or with berry jam. This recipe produces a most wonderful baba. However, if all conditions are not just right, it can be a sticky mess.
Serves 6–8

WITH APRICOTS

150 g apricots, stoned and cooked
150 g sugar
10 eggs, separated
150 g butter

Puree apricots and add sugar. Beat well. The puree should be light yellow colour.

In another bowl, gradually beat egg yolks into the butter. Add to puree.

Beat egg whites till stiff. Fold into mixture and mix well.

Place in a well greased, floured loaf tin the same as is used for kulich (see recipe), and bake in a 180°C (350°F) oven for 45 minutes.

KHVOROST

1 egg
30 g sugar
150 mL milk
2 cups flour
½ teaspoon salt
oil for deep frying
500 g icing sugar

Beat egg with sugar. Stir in milk. Sift flour with salt and mix in to form a stiff dough. Roll out on a floured board. Cut into strips about 10 cm long and 3 cm wide. Make a slit as in the diagram and knead one half through the slit.

Deep-fry in hot oil. Put 3 or 4 in to fry at one time till golden brown. Drain. Place icing sugar in sifter. Sift over pastry after it is fried but before it gets cold. Will keep 1–2 weeks if kept in a dry airtight container.
Serves 8–10

Khvorost

1 Cut pastry into strips 10 cm long by 3 cm wide and make a slit in centre

2 Turn half through the slit as shown then deep-fry

Khvorost

CHOCOLATE TORTE
TORT SHOKOLADNYI

5 eggs, separated
200 g sugar
270 g dark cooking chocolate, melted
½ teaspoon vanilla essence
70 g flour, sifted
1 teaspoon bicarbonate of soda
½ teaspoon cream of tartar
70 g toasted almonds, finely chopped

CREAM
100 g sugar
80 mL milk
200 g butter
1 tablespoon cocoa powder
½ teaspoon cognac

CHOCOLATE GLAZE
1 cup sugar
60–80 g unsalted butter
2 tablespoons cocoa powder
1 tablespoon milk

Beat egg yolks vigorously with 160 g sugar until creamy, add 170 g melted chocolate and the vanilla and mix well.

In another mixing bowl, whip egg whites until stiff with 40 g sugar and add to chocolate mixture. Fold in flour; bicarbonate of soda, cream of tartar and remaining chocolate.

Prepare baking tray by lining the surface with greaseproof paper. Pour mixture onto greaseproof paper. Bake in a moderate oven at 180°C (350°F) for 30–40 minutes.

To make cream, mix sugar and milk until sugar is dissolved. Add butter, cocoa and cognac and beat well until mixture is smooth.

When cake is cool, cut in half and spread with prepared cream, using a wet knife to spread. Then stack one piece on top of the other.

To make chocolate glaze, beat sugar with butter until sugar has dissolved. Mix cocoa and milk together in a cup and add to the butter mixture. Beat until smooth then spread on cake using a spatula. Cover the whole torte with cream and sprinkle with almonds or chocolate caraque (see recipe).

CHOCOLATE CARAQUE
120 g cooking chocolate

Grate chocolate onto a warmed plate placed over a saucepan of hot water. When melted, spread on marble or on a metal baking tray which has been refrigerated.

When chocolate has set, scrape off into pieces with a sharp knife or a melon baller.

RUSSIAN TORTE
TORT RUSSKI

5 eggs
3 tablespoons sugar
1 cup flour, sifted

FILLING
2 egg yolks
150 mL milk
1 tablespoon flour
100 g sugar
450 mL cream
10 g gelatine, softened in 3
   tablespoons warm water
1 tablespoon rum
½ teaspoon vanilla essence

CREAM
150 mL cream
3 tablespoons sugar

Beat eggs with sugar. Warm the mixture a little by placing the bowl in a container of hot water for a few minutes. Beat well and heat again. Beat again then fold in flour carefully. The heating produces a drier pastry than otherwise.

Line a baking tray with greaseproof paper and pour batter so that it is evenly spread. Bake in a 180°C (350°F) oven for approximately 20 minutes.
Caution: Start watching the pastry colour after 15 minutes. A slight variation in egg mixture temperature can change the cooking times.

To make filling, beat the egg yolks into the milk and add flour and 2 tablespoons sugar, mixing well.

In another bowl whip cream combined with remaining 60 g sugar and pour into the yolk mixture. Mix lightly. Add gelatine, rum and vanilla and beat until smooth.

To make cream, refrigerate the cream for 10 minutes. Then add sugar and mix well so that sugar is dissolved. Beat until thick.

To serve, when the pastry has cooled, divide into 3 equal layers. Cover with filling. Stack layers on top of one another and cover the sides with filling. Decorate top with cream.
Serves 6–8

Chocolate Torte

Chocolate Caraque

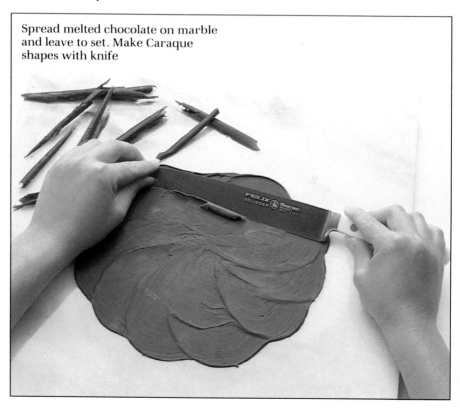

Spread melted chocolate on marble and leave to set. Make Caraque shapes with knife

DESSERTS

STRAWBERRY TART
PIROZHNOE KLUBNICHNOE

60 g butter
1 egg, separated
1 tablespoon grated lemon rind
170 g flour, sifted
1 ½ tablespoons sugar
1 teaspoon bicarbonate of soda
200 mL whipped cream
¼ teaspoon vanilla
180 g red fruit–flavoured jelly crystals
500 g strawberries

Combine in a saucepan, butter, egg yolk and lemon rind and heat gently. Remove from heat, add flour, sugar and bicarbonate of soda and beat. Place container in refrigerator for 30 minutes.

Roll dough out on a floured board, about 8 mm thick and big enough to cover a baking tray. Grease tray. Carefully lift pastry into tray finishing off the corners and edges neatly.

Bake in a 180°C (350°F) oven 25–30 minutes until golden. When cool, cut pastry in half, and spread cream to which vanilla has been added. Spread a little more cream on one half than the other. This will be the bottom half. Place the other on top.

Add water to jelly crystals according to directions on packet. Allow to cool but not set.

Arrange strawberries on top of cream on top layer and pour jelly over the fruit. Place in refrigerator until jelly has set.
Serves 4–6

PASKHA
PASKHA

1.5 kg cottage cheese
250 g unsalted butter, softened
100 g candied peel
½ teaspoon vanilla essence
2 cups thickened cream
5 eggs, hard-boiled and finely chopped
200–250 g sugar, sifted
100 g blanched almonds, finely chopped
100 g sultanas

Place cottage cheese in a colander, covering it with a small plate and pressing it down with a heavy weight to drain. Then rub cheese through a fine sieve with the back of a spoon.

In a mixing bowl beat butter with cheese.

In a small dish mix candied peel and vanilla and allow to soak. Add cream to cheese mixture and mix well with a wooden spoon.

Add chopped eggs to the mixture and beat well. Add 200 g of sugar and taste. Add more sugar if desirable. Fold in remaining ingredients and beat till smooth. It should be the consistency of a thick cream.

Traditionally, a special mould is used, but a flowerpot with a drain hole will be just as good. The pot should be approximately 25 cm or a little taller and approximately 15 cm at its base. Line the clean pot with a double layer of dampened cheesecloth, which is considerably longer than the pot.

Spoon mixture into the cheesecloth, pressing in to eliminate air pockets. Fold the cheesecloth to close the open end.

Place the pot in a soup plate or a similar container and weigh down the mixture. Cans of food are suitable for this. Place the whole assembly into the refrigerator overnight or longer.

To serve, invert pot and unwrap cheesecloth. The result should be a thick rich pyramid–shaped icecream-like mixture. Traditionally it was eaten at Easter with kulich. It will keep refrigerated for about 1 week.
Serves 12

CHARLOTTE RUSSE
SHARLOTKA

20–25 sponge fingers or boudoir biscuits
6 egg yolks
120 g sugar
350 mL milk
½ teaspoon vanilla essence
2 teaspoons gelatine softened in 3 tablespoons water
½ cup cold sour cream
½ cup cold whipped cream

RASPBERRY OR STRAWBERRY PUREE
1 kg fruit
2 tablespoon sugar
¼ cup Kirsch or other berry liqueur

Choose a charlotte mould or the largest round cake tin available. Line the bottom with biscuits which have been shaped so that they are wider at one end than the other.

Arrange so that tapered end is towards the middle or so biscuits overlap and there are no gaps. Stand the remainder of the biscuits vertically, close together so that there are no gaps.

In a mixing bowl, beat egg yolks till thick, add sugar and continue beating vigorously until mixture is a thick but runny consistency. Heat milk with added vanilla until the first small bubbles appear on the side of the saucepan. Immediately but slowly, pour milk into egg mixture continually beating. Then return mixture to saucepan. Scrape pan with wooden spoon or a spatula. Heat again stirring constantly until it thickens. *Do not boil.*

Remove custard from heat. Add gelatine mixture and stir well so that it dissolves. Whip creams until thick and stir into custard.

Cover bowl with a cloth and refrigerate for 30 minutes, stirring a few times until custard is the consistency of cold honey. Pour this mixture into the biscuit mould. Refrigerate overnight.

To make puree, place fruit in a large mixing bowl and squash with the back of a mixing spoon or spatula. Cover with sugar to taste and add liqueur.

Cover with greaseproof paper or plastic wrap and refrigerate for a few hours until the sugar has been coloured by the fruit.

To serve, if the custard did not fill biscuit mould, then top up with fruit puree. Otherwise serve separately.

Invert the serving plate on top of the mould and flip both over to invert. The mould should come off easily unless there were cracks in the biscuit mould and custard has stuck to the side. In that case, use a wet knife to ease off any difficult areas. To reinforce the free standing mould, tie a 10 cm wide red ribbon around the Charlotte and finish with a big bow.

Serves 8–10

RUM SOUFFLE
SUFLE ROMOVOE

250 g butter
200 g caster sugar
16 egg yolks
150 g ground almonds
1 teaspoon lemon peel
10 egg whites
½ cup rum or cognac, warmed

Cream butter and sugar till smooth. Add egg yolks, ground almonds and lemon peel. Beat well.

In a separate mixing bowl, whip egg whites till stiff. Fold into butter mixture. Spoon the mixture into a souffle dish.

Bake in a 180°C (350°F) oven for 30 minutes until well risen. Remove from oven cautiously. Knocking it can cause the souffle to sink.

When slightly cooled, pour over warmed alcohol. Serve immediately.
Serves 4–6

Charlotte Russe

SWEETS

Kisel is a type of fruit jelly. Instead of gelatine for thickening, potato flour is used. If unavailable, substitute arrowroot. This produces a beautiful smooth, clear and refreshing kisel. Cornflour is not an acceptable alternative because the dish becomes opaque and has a different texture and taste.

Kisel can be made from berries or other fruits — fresh, frozen or dried. It can also be made from milk or fruit syrups and can be eaten hot or cold.

Russian ice-cream is world famous. It is smooth, rich and creamy. In the recipes, cream could be substituted for milk but it is then very high in fat.

CRANBERRY KISEL
KISEL KLYUKVENNYI

300 g cranberries
550 mL water, boiled and cooled
2 tablespoons potato flour
150 g sugar

Wash cranberries thoroughly and remove any stems. Place in a colander and pour boiling water over them, then drain.

In a mixing bowl, mash cranberries thoroughly. Add 100 mL water. Mix and mash. Put through a sieve and press pulp with the back of a spoon, reserving the juice.

Add 450 mL water to strained pulp in a saucepan and bring to the boil. Boil for 2–3 minutes, then pour off 100 mL and strain the mixture through a sieve. Cool and add the potato flour, mixing well till dissolved.

Allow the remainder to keep boiling until the fruit has totally disintegrated. Add sugar while it is boiling and stir until dissolved.

Cool slightly. Strain through a sieve. Add potato flour mixture. Bring to the boil stirring constantly until mixture thickens slightly. Add reserved juice and stir well. Pour into individual serving dishes to set.
Serves 4–6

ROSELLA KISEL

1 kg rosella (see Note)
200 mL water
400 g sugar
2½ tablespoons potato flour

Wash rosella very well and separate petals from seed. Add both to water in a saucepan and bring to the boil. Boil gently until volume of water has reduced by half. Strain through a sieve. Remove seeds and mash the remaining pulp with the back of a spoon, pressing sieve well so that all juice is removed. Discard pulp and seeds. Add sugar to juice. Refrigerate for a few hours.

Add potato flour to mixture. Bring to the boil, stirring constantly. Pour into individual serving dishes to set.
Note: Rosella is the edible, fleshy flower of the Rosella or Jamaica Sorrel plant. It is usually red but sometimes yellow, and is sometimes used for preserving in the form of jams and jellies.
Serves 4–6

WATERMELON KISEL
KISEL IZ ARBUZA

800 g pink watermelon pulp
100 g sugar
2½ tablespoons potato flour
100 mL water, boiled and cooled

Put watermelon through an electric juicer to separate juice from seeds. Add sugar to juice.

Dissolve potato flour in water and bring to the boil, stirring. Add watermelon juice. Bring to the boil again, stirring constantly. Pour into individual serving dishes to set.
Serves 4–6

Variation:

STRAWBERRY KISEL
KISEL IZ KLUBNIKI

200 g strawberries
200 g sugar
2½ tablespoons potato flour
2 cups water, boiled and cooled

Wash and clean strawberries removing any damaged parts. Place in a bowl, pour on sugar and refrigerate for a few hours.

Strain through a sieve, mashing pulp with the back of a spoon. Reserve the juice and discard remaining pulp.

Dissolve potato flour in water in a saucepan and bring to the boil, stirring. Add strawberry juice. Bring to the boil again stirring constantly till slightly thickened. Pour into individual serving dishes to set and serve with extra strawberries.
Serves 4–6

GRAPE KISEL
KISEL IZ VINOGRADA

300 g grapes
150 g sugar
2½ tablespoons potato flour
2 cups water, boiled and cooled

Wash grapes well and put through an electric juicer. This will squeeze out the juice very efficiently, leaving skins and pips. Add sugar.

Dissolve potato flour in water in a saucepan and bring to the boil. Add grape juice, stirring constantly. Bring to the boil. Pour into individual serving dishes to set.
Serves 4–6

Strawberry Kisel

LEMON SORBET
LIMONNOE MOROZHENOE

4 lemons
2 cups sugar
1.25 litres water

Peel lemons, remove pith and seeds. Finely chop pulp and mix with sugar. Let stand for 2 hours.

Add water and heat slowly, stirring constantly until sugar dissolves.

Pour into freezer trays or other suitable containers and freeze for 1 hour.

Remove from freezer. Beat vigorously for 2 minutes. Pour back into trays and freeze.
Serves 6–8

WINE SORBET
MOROZHENOE IZ VINA

1 cup sugar
1 teaspoon lemon rind
14 egg yolks
2 cups white wine

Add 2½ tablespoons sugar to lemon rind in a mixing bowl. Stand for 15 minutes.

Add remaining sugar and egg yolks and beat well until thick. Gradually mix in white wine.

Pour into freezer trays or other suitable containers and freeze for 1 hour.

Remove from freezer. Beat vigorously for 3–5 minutes. Pour back into trays and freeze.
Serves 6–8

ICE CREAM (1)
MOROZHENOE

20 egg yolks
2 cups sugar
½ teaspoon vanilla essence
1.5 litres milk

Beat egg yolks with sugar until creamy. Add vanilla. Stir in milk. Transfer to a saucepan and bring just to the boil, until the first few bubbles appear on the surface. Cool.

Pour into trays or other suitable dishes and place in freezer for 1 hour.

Remove from freezer and beat ice cream vigorously for 3–5 minutes. Pour back into trays and freeze.
Serves 8–10

Variation:

CHOCOLATE ICE CREAM
SHOKOLADNOE MOROZHENOE

Add to (1):
100 g cooking chocolate, melted
2½ tablespoons cocoa powder
1 cup milk

After milk–egg mixture has been heated and cooled, add melted chocolate and cocoa dissolved in milk. Mix well and pour into freezer trays and continue as for (1).

Vanilla Ice Cream

DRINKS

KVAS

Kvas is a refreshing and mild home-brewed beer (about 1% alcohol) which is drunk by both children and adults at meal times. Essentially kvas is a mixture of water, bread and usually malt made into a dough or mash then left to ferment. This fermented substance is then mixed with more water and yeast, sugar and other flavouring ingredients and left to ferment further. The flavouring for kvas can be from fruit or berry juices, including blackcurrant, lemon, raspberry, strawberry, apple, raisin and pear. These flavourings are sometimes spiced with ginger or mint.

1 kg fried or toasted breadcrumbs
5 litres water, boiling
25 g yeast
200 g sugar
1 tablespoon mint, finely chopped
50 g raisins

In a large container, cover breadcrumbs with boiling water. Cover with a cloth and set aside for 3–4 hours. Strain. Dissolve yeast in a cup or small dish in a little warm water. Add to breadcrumb liquid and mix with a wooden spoon. Mix in sugar and mint. Cover with a cloth and set aside to brew for 5–6 hours.

During this time prepare bottles and tops. If tops cannot be clamped, arrange to secure them with thin wire as for champagne. Bottles and tops must be sterilized with boiling water.

After standing, strain liquid again. The finer the strainer, the clearer the final product. Into each bottle put a few raisins and pour liquid into prepared bottles. Seal and cap.

Place bottles in a cool, dark place for 2–3 days. The kvas should then be ready.

Refrigerate before serving in glasses as for ginger beer or use for soup base.
Makes 10 × 500 mL bottles

LEMON KVAS

1 lemon
2 litres water
100 g sugar
lemon essence
lemon colouring
10 g yeast
approximately ½ cup raisins

Grate lemon rind and squeeze the juice from the lemon. Combine rind and juice with water and bring to the boil. Add sugar, mix and cool. Add a few drops of lemon essence and colouring.

Dissolve yeast in a cup in a little warm water and add to mixture. Prepare bottles and tops. If tops cannot be clamped, arrange to secure them with thin wire as for champagne. Bottles and tops must be sterilized with boiling water.

Strain liquid. Add a few raisins to each bottle and pour liquid into bottles. Leave opened for 2–3 hours in a warm place. As soon as the mixture begins brewing, immediately clamp on the top. Brewing can be identified by the appearance of bubbles and/or froth on the surface. Remove bottles to a cool dark place for 1–2 days. Refrigerate before serving.
Makes 5 × 500 ml bottles

TEA–BASED PUNCH
PUNSH IZ CHAYA

2 lemons
4 oranges
2 cups sugar
1 cup cognac
1.5 litres tea, hot

Grate lemon and orange rind and grind with sugar with a pestle or the back of a spoon. Add lemon and orange juice, cognac, and hot tea. Blend well. Reheat and serve.
Makes 8 glasses

WINE PUNCH
PUNSH IZ VINA

2 cups sugar
1 teaspoon grated lemon rind
2 litres white wine
100 mL rum or cognac

Add sugar to lemon rind and grind with a pestle or the back of a spoon to release lemon oils.

Place in a saucepan, add wine and boil, stirring constantly until sugar has dissolved.

Punch is drunk hot. Add rum or cognac just before serving so that alcohol does not evaporate.
Makes 2 litres

Kvas

1 Place breadcrumbs and boiling water in a large container; cover with muslin cloth and set aside

2 Add yeast, sugar and mint

3 Pour strained Kvas into prepared bottle with raisins

FOR YOUR INFORMATION

Glossary of Terms

AUSTRALIA	UK	USA
Equipment and terms		
can	tin	can
crushed	minced	pressed
frying pan	frying pan	skillet
grill	grill	broil
greaseproof paper	greaseproof paper	waxproof paper
paper towel	kitchen paper	white paper towel
plastic wrap	cling film	plastic wrap
punnet	punnet	basket for 250 g fruit
seeded	stoned	pitted
Ingredients		
bacon rasher	bacon rasher	bacon slice
beetroot	beetroot	beets
black olive	black olive	ripe olive
capsicum	pepper	sweet pepper
cornflour	cornflour	cornstarch
cream	single cream	light or coffee cream
crystallised fruit	crystallised fruit	candied fruit
eggplant	aubergine	eggplant
flour	plain flour	all-purpose flour
green cabbage	white or roundhead cabbage	cabbage
pawpaw	papaya	papaya or papaw
prawn	prawn or shrimp	shrimp
shallot	spring onion	scallion
snow pea	mangetout, sugar pea	snow pea
sour cream	soured cream	dairy sour cream
stock cube	stock cube	bouillon cube
tasty cheese	mature Cheddar	Cheddar
rich cream	double cream	heavy or whipping cream
tomato puree	tomato puree	tomato paste
tomato sauce	tomato sauce	tomato ketchup
unsalted butter	unsalted butter	sweet butter
wholemeal flour	wholemeal flour	wholewheat flour
yoghurt	natural yoghurt	unflavoured yoghurt
zucchini	courgette	zucchini

If you need to substitute

Crispbread: replace with crackers or French toasts.
Fresh fruit: replace with canned or tinned fruit.
Fresh herbs: replace with a quarter of the recommended quantity of dried herbs.
Lebanese cucumbers: also called English, telegraph or Cypress cucumbers. Replace with any smooth-skinned cucumber.
Mulberries: replace with blackcurrants.
Pecans: replace with walnuts.
Rock melons: replace with honeydew melons.
Snapper: replace with any firm white fish such as haddock, cod or whiting.

Oven Temperatures

Celsius	Fahrenheit	
120	250	Very slow
140–150	275–300	Slow
		Moderately slow
160	325	Moderate
180	350	Moderately hot
190	375	Hot
200	400	
220	425	
230	450	Very hot
250–260	475–500	

Measurements

Standard Metric Measures

1 cup	=	250 mL
1 tablespoon	=	20 mL
1 teaspoon	=	5 mL

All spoon measurements are level

Cup Measures

1 × 250 mL cup =	Grams	Ounces
breadcrumbs, dry	125	4½
soft	60	2
butter	250	8¾
cheese, grated		
cheddar	125	4½
coconut, desiccated	95	3¼
flour, cornflour	130	4¾
plain or self-raising	125	4½
wholemeal	135	4¾
fruit, mixed dried	160	5¾
honey	360	12¾
sugar, caster	225	7¾
crystalline	250	8¾
icing	175	6¾
moist brown	170	6
nuts	125	4

INDEX

ACKNOWLEDGEMENTS

The publisher would like to thank the
following for providing cutlery, glassware and
tableware for the photography of this book:

Accoutrement Cook Shop, Mosman for
tableware (page 31)
Dansab Pty Ltd for cutlery (page 28)
Mikasa Tableware for tableware and cutlery
(pages 20, 23, 27, 38, 45, 87)
Royal Doulton Australia Pty Ltd for tableware
(pages 25, 28, 33, 35, 37, 42, 57, 59, 61, 65, 82,
85)
Sasaki for cutlery (pages 53, 82, 91)
Wedgwood Australia Limited for tableware
(pages 16, 38, 46, 49, 50, 53, 55, 56, 62, 71, 73)